THE BUDAPEST FILE

Books by George Szirtes

POETRY

The Slant Door (Secker & Warburg, 1979)
November and May (Secker & Warburg, 1981)
Short Wave (Secker & Warburg, 1984)
The Photographer in Winter (Secker & Warburg, 1986)
Metro (OUP, 1988)
Bridge Passages (OUP, 1991)
Blind Field (OUP, 1994)
Selected Poems 1976-1996 (OUP, 1996)
The Red All Over Riddle Book [for children] (Faber, 1997)
Portrait of my Father in an English Landscape (OUP, 1998)
A Modern Bestiary, with artist Ana Maria Pacheco
    (Pratt Contemporary Art, 2000)
The Budapest File (Bloodaxe Books / Corvina, 2000)

TRANSLATION

Imre Madách: *The Tragedy of Man* [verse play]
    (Corvina / Puski, 1989)
Sándor Csoóri: *Barbarian Prayer: Selected Poems* (Corvina 1989)
István Vas: *Through the Smoke: Selected Poems* (Corvina, 1989)
Dezső Kosztolányi: *Anna Édes* [novel] (Quartet, 1991)
Ottó Orbán: *The Blood of the Walsungs: Selected Poems* (Bloodaxe
    Books / Corvina, 1993)
Zsuzsa Rakovszky: *New Life: Selected Poems* (OUP, 1994)
The Colonnade of Teeth: Modern Hungarian Poetry, with George
    Gömöri (Bloodaxe Books, 1996)
The Lost Rider: Hungarian Poetry 16-20th Century (Corvina, 1998)
Gyula Krúdy: *The Adventures of Sindbad* [short stories] (CEUP, 1999)
László Krasznahorkai: *The Melancholy of Resistance* (Quartet, 1999)

AS EDITOR

Freda Downie: *Collected Poems* (Bloodaxe Books, 1995)

George Szirtes

THE
BUDAPEST
FILE

CORVINA

BLOODAXE BOOKS

Copyright © George Szirtes 1979, 1981, 1984, 1986,
1988, 1991, 1994, 1996, 1998, 2000
Cover and section page pictures: Clarissa Upchurch

ISBN: 1 85224 531 X Bloodaxe Books
963 13 4914 4 Corvina Books

First published 2000 by
Bloodaxe Books Ltd,
P.O. Box 1SN,
Newcastle upon Tyne NE99 1SN.

Published in Hungary by
Corvina Books,
Vörösmarty tér 1,
Budapest H-1051.

Bloodaxe Books Ltd acknowledges
the financial assistance of Northern Arts.

Cover printing by J. Thomson Colour Printers Ltd, Glasgow.

Printed in Great Britain by
Cromwell Press Ltd, Trowbridge, Wiltshire.

To the memory of my mother,

MAGDALENA SZIRTES / NUSSBACHER MAGDALENA
1924-1975

and to my father,

LESLIE SZIRTES / SZIRTES LÁSZLÓ

NOTE & ACKNOWLEDGEMENTS

Most of these poems were first collected in these earlier books: *The Slant Door* (1979), *November and May* (1981), *Short Wave* (1984) and *The Photographer in Winter* (1986), published by Secker & Warburg; and *Metro* (1988), *Bridge Passages* (1991), *Blind Field* (1994), *Selected Poems 1976-1996* (1996) and *Portrait of My Father in an English Landscape* (1998), published by Oxford University Press.

Also included in this selection are two recent poems written to commission for radio. 'Lullaby of Broadway' was set against the dance sequence of that name from Busby Berkeley's *Gold Diggers* of 1935. As will appear from other poems, Berkeley's choreography has long fascinated me. I find it beautiful, kitsch and disturbing at the same time. It seems to me a vivid footnote to European history and so much more. The radio poem, which ran for about 20 minutes, expanded and dramatised this hunch.

The other commission, 'The Lost Scouts', was the product of a visit to the triennial reunion of the surviving members of my father's scout troop. Being Jewish most of them died in the war and many went into emigration. After 1989, they began to gather round a camp fire outside Budapest, to sing songs and tell stories. They still do so, coming from all parts of the world to be together for a few days every three years. In September 1999, I accompanied them on their last reunion, taped the campfire and several interviews. I wrote a newspaper article using some of the material but the core of it went into the poem, which employed the noises and voices I recorded. I would like to thank the BBC for the opportunity to write both programmes.

A number of new poems appear in this selection, mostly sonnet sequences written over the last two years. Some of them have appeared in *Ambit*, *The Hungarian Quarterly* or been broadcast by the BBC.

G.Sz.

CONTENTS

The Flies

PREFACE

This is a curious and somewhat surprising book. I hardly knew it existed until I set about compiling it following a discussion with my publisher. I hadn't realised I had written so much that was so intrinsically wound up with a subject whose epicentre is Hungary but whose domain is essentially eastern continental Europe, more particularly the history of that region, which is by extension the history of the circumstances that made my grandparents, parents, myself – and even my children – what we are. The subject therefore, the principle of organisation, is history, and the poems are arranged according to the historical period they deal with, from the inter-war period to the present. This is not the result of a grand original scheme as the poems themselves were written at various times without any specific theme in mind and it is only now, some 20 years after, that the shape of that history becomes apparent to me so that I see it as a constant shadow.

My family was among the large number of refugees that left Hungary following the 1956 uprising. There had been previous waves of migration: in the period following the Ottoman invasion in the 16th century; under Habsburg rule in the 18th century; following the revolution of 1848; near the end of the 19th century; after the First World War; in the anti-semitic period of the 1930s; after the Second World War at the time of the communist take-over; and then, lastly, in my family's time. Refugees left in various circumstances with various forms of baggage. My father, mother, younger brother and I were part of a group of about twenty who walked across the border into Austria by night. The fields were muddy. We arrived without luggage, except for a small case of photographs that I still possess. One suitcase had been given in fee to those who guided us across and the other was lost on the walk. I lost a shoe on the way.

After three days in an Austrian refugee camp we were offered a flight to England. We landed at night at Heathrow, spent a few days at an army camp at Tidworth (the troops might still have been out in Suez at the time), and were then transferred to an off-season boarding house in Westgate, Kent. This was a week or two before Christmas 1956. In the spring of 1957 we moved up to London where my father and mother found work and we began our English education. At the time of our departure only my father spoke English but, out of sheer necessity, we disciplined ourselves to speak it at home. In the meantime we were moving around north-west London. My parents tried to get an assisted passage to Australia where my father had a cousin, but my mother, a concentration camp survivor, had a weak heart and failed the medical, so the idea had to be abandoned.

Once settled here, England was simply the place where we lived. I read English books, had English friends, watched English TV and went on English holidays. Later, in my teens, when I began to write, it did not occur to me to write in Hungarian: it was far more natural to write in English, the language in which I thought and felt. As an 'A' level scientist, my reading of literature was uncontrolled and undisciplined. I was impressed, as many kids of my age in the 60s were, by the Beats and the Liverpool Poets, but also by the Penguin Modern European Poets series, and by odd corners of English Romanticism. It was an eclectic mixture that nowhere included the mainstream. It was only once I had changed course, gone to art college (much against the wishes of my parents) and met Martin Bell, that I was introduced to the wider map of contemporary poetry in English. I still regard Bell himself as one of the most brilliant and underrated poets of the post-war period.

In the five years between leaving education and my first book, the focus and manner of my writing changed. The suicide of my mother in 1975 was the trigger. It released a great complex of feelings I had to learn to pick my way through. Whereas before I had written wholly on the spur of the moment and trusted instinctively to my ability to generate dream-like images, I now became aware of learning a craft, of the importance of observation and distance. The immediate results were strange and pedestrian, and the learning painful, but I am more than ever certain that it was necessary. I needed to learn when to hold back and when to let go. I needed to create bigger, firmer structures to accommodate and support the incoherent images I had grown up with, and to anchor them in a narrative or historical process. The later long poems would have been impossible without this period of readjustment, and in any case my temperament and instinct demanded it. One does what one has to in these circumstances.

Despite this, there was very little about Hungary in my first two books. A few poems, such as 'At the Dressing-table Mirror', were based on incidents in Hungary, but their locations were intimate spaces arising from the no-man's-land of childhood memory. There was no ground plan and no street map. If the awareness of

Hungary as a specific point of reference existed at all it was only as a faint pulse on the radar.

I think now I was like a beginner, trying to master a kind of inner cartography. Eight years after my mother's death the map was still crude but there was enough of it available to make a visit to Budapest seem like a natural step. I had some idea where I was going. I had spent hour after hour, over several years, talking to my father on tape about his own life, and had read a little for myself on the history of Central Europe.

My return coincided with the appearance of my third book, *Short Wave*. The visit surpassed my expectations and changed everything all over again. It was an intense, almost hallucinatory experience. Many poems came out of it, including two of my longer sequences, *The Photographer in Winter* (which was to be the title of the book that followed) and *The Courtyards*. There was a new subject-matter, a new state of mind, a new notion of structure in view.

The visit also changed the direction of my professional life. By 1984 I had all but forgotten the language of my childhood, but now it began slowly to return, a process accelerated by the work of translation I was immediately encouraged to undertake. Soon I no longer had time for painting or drawing. All the time I had devoted to that was taken up by translation, but I was glad. Translation provided me with another education, a partial living, and a constant drip of new materials and new voices for my own poetry. It also created the sense of shift that a historical map requires. I don't think the half-haunted polyphony of *Metro* would have been possible without it.

I returned every year for shorter or longer periods. The first shock wore off, as things do and the visits became more routine but still productive. The figure of my mother was no longer as isolated as it had been at the time of her death.

At this point something else occurred which forced everyone to change maps, politically, psychologically and in many other, as yet unclear, ways. I spent most of 1989 in Hungary as a British Council scholar – I have often had cause to be grateful to the British Council – writing, translating, walking, talking, listening, attending meetings and demonstrations, scarcely believing what was happening. The political system was in the process of collapse and every week brought something new and unexpected to our attention. It was an intense and productive time, as exciting as any I had known, but psychologically stressful in ways I could hardly articulate to myself and still find difficult.

If it brought anything home to me it was that my work should try to give some shape to the experience of individual survival in adverse social conditions. One poem in the 1991 book, *Bridge Passages*, 'A Game of Statues', imagined people after the war returning to their homes, entering their rooms and passing straight through the walls, turning into statues in the process. The elevations of Budapest buildings are teeming with figures. A city full of living statues seemed a potent and appropriate image for survival. I wanted to create such statues in verse.

Most of the poems in *Bridge Passages* – the title was not a clever pun as someone suggested but a pretty desperate attempt on my part to discover bridges between my life in England and my history in Hungary – constitute a kind of reportage based on the events of that year, a reportage in which journalism is experienced as poetry. The obligation to history at this point was particularly divisive. Everything was crying out for definition or redefinition, but the triangular relationship between Hungary, myself and England felt all the more uncomfortable for it being defined at all. None of the three parties involved knew how it felt about the other two.

It was about this time that the search for my mother began to be superseded by the search for my father, who was, and is, still alive. The transition is represented by the 1994 collection, *Blind Field*, ostensibly a book about photographs and photography but actually about images of frozen time and the dramatic intervention in this of my mother, who had herself been a photographer. In that book I identified some aspects of her with the photographer of the extreme, Diane Arbus, who is the off-stage subject of a number of poems in the book. The longest poem, 'Transylvana', is the record of a visit to Romania, to see my mother's birthplace and her one surviving relative (called Virgil in the poem), but it is also the registering of a cultural shock at what I saw there. Like the poems in *Bridge Passages*, 'Transylvana' is in many respects a highly photo-journalistic poem. 'He don't *invent* it,' as Peter Reading says of his own reporting of the grotesque or the distressing in *Ukulele Music*. Of course he is right: most poets don't.

The history of my mother took me to Hungary: the history of my father has drawn me back. I have spent 43 of my 51 years in England. My father spoke some English before he left Hungary, the only one of us to do so. I have watched him grow older, seen his name anglicised to Surtees at work then de-anglicised again since his retirement. I have seen him move through the suburbs

14

of London, remarry and return to Hungary with his old scout associates. His journey, like mine, has been through culture and language. Above all, his has been through history. That history is part of the English landscape now. The three long sonnet sequences of *Portrait of My Father in an English Landscape* are my attempts to place, realise and annotate his journey as a human document.

Such enterprises clarify in retrospect. A poet has broad desires and ambitions but they rarely approximate to full programmes. The process of writing continually modifies and re-directs intention. I did not set out to "write" either Hungary or England. These national (let alone nationalistic) concepts are incidental, and often, to my mind, harmful. Becoming aware of places as background subjects inevitably brought them into the foreground, but their advance into fuller consciousness was accompanied, for me, by a growing realisation of a third, and possibly more pervasive theme, which threatened to negate both places.

My greatest difficulty with nationally or culturally rooted notions is that they inevitably exclude those who are migrants, floaters, drifters and shadows. I may envy the rooted but I cannot enter their territory. What sense would it make for me to write like W.N. Herbert, or Tony Harrison, or Seamus Heaney, or a Liverpudlian or a Londoner or an East Anglian? I cannot even write as a Buda-pester. Writers like me cannot intrude into such specificity. This represents a certain loss. Our language may strive for vigour but it will always have an air of the synthetic. I am aware of this even as I am writing now. There is nothing honest that can be done to "mend" this, and poetry is, in the end, a matter of honesty. The tribeless cannot simply put on the appropriate headdress. It is not Hungary or any other place that is the issue. It is the inbetween-ness. The synthesis is its own voice. I think my constant engage-ment with devices like pun, metre and rhyme is a way of exercising and testing that synthesis. I would like to bring together desire, tenderness, fear and wit (and fear and wit are often closer than we are led to think) to lend structure to disparate experiences I cannot flavour with the vibrancy of a local diction.

I wish I could. Poetry is always local. It is just that in this case – and in the case of other writers, indeed, I would suggest an increasing number of writers, those used to moving about from place to place without a secure notion of belonging – the notion of the local is rooted in the incidental. For diction we might well substitute form as some kind of driving necessity. Hence, perhaps, the obsessional form-making of the Hungarian sonnet sequences.

Hence also, at the same time, the conscious attempt to break against that form, to run sentences against lines, but to keep rediscovering the line, the rhyme, the integral pattern against which the sprawl of experience can be mapped. Hence the narrative and anecdotal patterns that constitute the forward forces of the poems.

Our private lives rarely run to grand patterns, and it takes a particular form of mythopoeia to see and form them that way. These 'Hungarian' poems appear to look to a phantasmal Budapest as their hub. It feels odd to have them separated from the other poems, a little painful too, like driving an axe down a fault line, but I can see it makes a kind of sense. In the same way the poems about England, or rather poems that turn out to be about England, sometimes more, sometimes less consciously, lie on the other side of the fault line. I think my project, if I have any, is to hold both sides together, even if only for my own sake. The bridge passages join two sides of the river and it is interesting (or 'not uninteresting' as I would have said in one of my 'English' modes) to examine the two banks. In this respect the retrospective/prospective 'project' is as much geography as history.

GEORGE SZIRTES

The Drowned Girl

(for Peter Porter)

Salt fogs insulate
The harbours, those fishing villages
Wood visited and painted:
Men wrestling after dark;

The white sea, and the tinkers
Arguing over a horse;
Rows of houses like waves,
Drowning in their solitude.

Your lips and tongue explore
These sounds; the spitting 'th',
'w' – the rolling silence of water,
The joyful crowned vowels –

These were the words I learnt
Quickest of all – monosyllabic,
Twisted to boys' threats
Like a collar twisted

Over a scrawny neck of land
The sea kisses and bites at.
These were and are the words
That I now teach my children.

*

She turned up in the cabin
Three centuries later; a girl
Some twenty years old, they say,
A mile off Anglesey.

The sleeping girl, broken
By a falling wardrobe,
Drifting among her
Ragged dresses, eyes

In perpetual surprise
That this sudden kiss
Should come with such sucking,
Such uncouth labials,

Stretches out her hand
To push away the swell
Under the door, and finds it
Kissed –

Soft, interminably soft.
Even in the white bone
This heart and hip cushion
My time and my words.

Drowned miles, bleached bones.
Earls of Meath or Ardglass.
Breasts locked in the cupboard:
Lockets boarded under waves.

                    *

But the low murmuring
Of the cabin expands
At last to music
Of other lives and other voices,

Meaning more dead than she did alive
To instruct my children
In the grammar of countries
Vaster, more important than theirs,

Yet with which they shall in time
Be themselves acquainted;
Thankless and hollow
Like this table or these bones;

Fortunate still in the choice
Of their father's adoptive home,
As was this English girl
In the salt noose, her birthright.

THE TOWN FLATTENED

war correspondence

The Yellow House at Eszterháza

You find it suddenly, opening up, then
quickly closing like the entrance to any estate.
The car zips by and it's gone. You've passed the gate
before you know it. You double back and when
you take stock properly a kind of gladness
moves you to admit it, just as you are admitted
into history or heritage, something perfectly fitted
to bring about the light and giddy madness
the peasant must have felt on seeing it
finished; that life like this is an extension
of the limits of the known world, beyond mention,
incomprehensible, almost infinite,
as if it were not the chains he had to wear
but something utterly sprightly, made of air.

Today, a room stuffed full of faience stoves
so white you'd think you were in a dove cot
and the doves ready to fly. Putti like tiny cloves
protruding from stucco, part of a lost plot
in which even seasons defer to the family name.
Tendrils gilded and twining, frescoes, glass
reflecting more glass, the great room's twists of flame
turned into icing. Before, ordinary grass,
ordinary shrubs, conducting a geometric
dance, the fountain dancing, the dwarf trees
marking time, but also dancing in parodies
of local custom, then performing a vanishing trick
into dusk, and Joseph Haydn, asleep
in the music room, thirty fathom deep.

The age of elegance is short. The broad
welcome in the curving wings, enlightened
stables, kitchens, the gentle patronising of awed
visitors, the courtesy shown to the frightened
soldier make just one generation. Then the show
moves on. The Chinese hangings swell
into dust. There are no fountains to overflow
the curling brim. No major domo rings the bell
for supper. Things easy come are easy gone.
So the opera house goes all to blazes.
A machine gun strafes the precious vases.
The puppet theatre turns grain store. No one
is going to be too bothered by any of this.
Let it remain in a state of decorous paralysis.

And then a miracle. A vehicle in the drive
has grown rococo horns as living proof
of loyalty. Meanwhile, the dead arrive
on a child's bike carried on the car roof.
Like all the punning dead they want their freedom.
Enormous faience doves have taken wing
and filled the room. Where have they come from?
How could I possibly offer them anything
but some notion of elegance, of what is humane,
enlightened, thirsted for, ridiculous?
Joseph Haydn in gentle Hungarian rain,
snuffing candles out for a good purpose,
releasing an orchestra. A molehill. A piece
of metal like a cartridge case under the trellis.

The Lukács Baths

1

It's circa 1900 and five women
have gathered here in semi-darkness
prepared to prophesy their own extinction.
The water shimmies down a pebbled wall,
a fountain hesitates. Their swimming costumes
are wasps' nests soaked through, softened by the gush,
their bathing caps are a green efflorescence.
They are the light at the bottom of deep pools
wobbling in uncomfortable sunshine
with rheumatic feet, imagining a Greece
ravaged by wars, prepared, they say, to sink.

2

Inside every grandmother there sits
an attractive young girl mouthing pieties,
complaining of sore lips or God knows what.
They prophesy the past with unerring accuracy;
history for them is painful gossip
half way between myth and memory.
They are on nodding terms with skeletons
who take the shape of husbands in dull rooms,
and they can tell the future as it shrinks
into its faint determined pattern.
It's hard to like them, harder to dislike them.
Their faces are light wrinkles in the water.

3

An enormous beech is jutting from the yard.
The walls, just as in crematoriums
are stuck with plaques in a handful of languages.
My shoulder's better. I can move my leg
God bless these healing waters. I can walk.
Inside and on the roof the swimsuits bulge.
I'm watching two old women as they swim
and push away the past like tired waves.

Grandfather's Dog

His hat would sometimes precede him into the hall.
These were the bad days when everything went wrong
and the smell of leather followed him like a stray dog
across the carpet. It was a ghostly creature that slunk
about the flat, settling on chairs and cushions;
all soft retentive things would take him in,
the children, the women. The dog of course had suffered,
such was its nature, and such was theirs, the children and women.

Because failure and humiliation are unexpected
the dog was to be expected. And sometimes it haunts me,
the thought of the dog. I've seen him sniffing
at my brother's ankles. His sheer size daunts me,
his dumb perseverance. I saw him once, sitting in the kitchen
beside my mother, under her feet, at his most
persevering. He ate her slowly and left not a bone,
so I knew him to be a bitter and vengeful ghost.

And grandfather, the factory hand, was likewise eaten,
by him first, then gas, right from the beginning.
Even now as I walk through the town it is there, sharp
and pervasive, a smell of leather-tanning.

The Town Flattened

1

This is Dada architecture; big stars of wood,
amulets of brick and a far church
blown down by the rational wind.
The whole town is like this. My hands
are so cold I can hardly write.
I am fascinated by their patterns though:
white walls and grandpapa dying
along with the cat and the chambermaid
(I only want a little bit of butter for my bread).

These stations are so draughty.
Were I a god I could rebuild all this in seven days.

2

Sun blurs the trees. Along the slats
light rattles like a carriage. The porch
sighs out another century but we maintain
our distance, preferring the panoramic
view afforded by this vacancy
between two paths. Surely if we touched
the trees they would sound like crystal.

3

My window eyes are brighter than a cat's.
I guard these trees with twigs and right-angles
and feel their hands upon my ivied walls,
a creeping caress. No one passes
to disturb our fusion except the servants
who keep the garden trim and wait for someone.

4

There should be a progression in all this.
My hands are so cold that I cannot write.
The whole town is reduced to rubble, like
remnants of a fire. I have walked the streets
and seen nothing but timber and fallen masonry.

You should not have sent the parcel on my dear.
I will let you know as soon as it arrives.

5

In the top room of an old hotel there sat
a spider sheltering from rain. It was
the biggest I had ever seen.
To tell the truth I dared not move
in case it scrambled down the wall.

There are draughts all over the place –
holes big enough to push a finger through.
Were these in walls you ask? Of a kind.
The wall of a head, the secret orchard
with its cobweb of hair. Amazing to think
strands like these can hold together
a wall, a thought, a family even.

6

The apples are burned red this year. In
every groove and ditch broken skins of apples
char the bank and the mist is a fine ash
caught between valleys.
                              But under it the idea of a skull
bearing the load of its leaves and branches,
pure, the dust cleansed off, and the thing
set on a table ready for inspection,
seems to contemplate the striking of a match,
a harvest.

The Accordionist

(for André Kertész)

The accordionist is a blind intellectual
carrying an enormous typewriter whose keys
grow wings as the instrument expands into a tall
horizontal hat that collapses with a tubercular wheeze.

My century is a sad one of collapses.
The concertina of the chest; the tubular bells
of the high houses; the flattened ellipses
of our skulls that open like petals.

We are the poppies sprinkled along the field.
We are simple crosses dotted with blood.
Beware the sentiments concealed
in this short rhyme. Be wise. Be good.

Eat Good Bread Dear Father

Every lunchtime they'd leave you a piece of *mignon*.
Now I can imagine the white of the paper bag
and the small yellow doily under the plate
in the afternoon half-dark. And I drag
from my memory not your room but mine
(or any room that seems to be half-dark)
to construct a world we may meet in. Here is the door
to the kitchen, here is the sideboard, the mark
on the tablecloth and the print of my thumb
on the page. Here nothing is known, everything dissolves
to noise or to music (but what is the difference?)
a music which says (so must mean) things, that solves
the pathos of cake on a saucer or the tiny
cosmic hum that rings an old woman's hand
as she moves in the kitchen like a conductor,
waving her notes into place, weaving the slender
sound of paper and footstep. We start as with lines
on a score, the *mignon* a radiance among other radiances,
with your blank childhood face and the space between lines
measuring distances.

The Lullaby of Broadway

We dance our way through nineteen thirty-five
down a *moderne* staircase into the heart of a ballroom.
The band is playing but no one else is in there.
It's nineteen thirty-five and they are waiting

for something to happen, for an army of pianos
to scoot and swivel towards them, or a pool to open
its petals under our feet and the girls to dive in,
for two lovers to kiss and a park to start singing

in a glossy routine to a poetry of numbers.
We're Gold Diggers of 1935
under the direction of Hollywood's Busby Berkeley
but it could be Eisenstein or Riefenstahl,

this year before Triumph of the Will,
the year of Italy in Abyssinia,
the year, in Russia, of Zinoviev,
a year of show trials, beatings, executions,

Gold Diggers all, in nineteen thirty-five,
still hoofing our way to darkness
in gorgeous giggles of satin and leather,
at the point of departure

on a balcony of the eleven-hundredth floor,
at the point when the dancing stops and the falling begins,
when the hauntings we invite begin to move as a body,
when we, the people, collude with the people's chorus

and all those notions of what it means to be a people,
stirred like hot coffee into a world of steam
and desire, right to the point of terror and heartbreak,
here at the point of departure.

*

This is the film, dear listener, I want you to imagine:
The film of the girl in the bed above the traffic,
dreamt by a man with a camera for an eye,
a single watcher in the night-time sky;

a watcher too in the rational and remorseless morning,
the hour of the journey to work that serves as a warning
to keep your pecker up as the jackboots march past you,
as the dizzying patterns you whirl in outlast you,

as the coffee boils over and the nipple strains in the cup,
as you watch the milk in the saucer when the kitten laps it up,
as darkness descends on the lampshade and the clock
and only dancers pass through the doors of the sleeping block.

*

Listener, listen: here's the sound of a city
before your time in a history turned dream
you recognise while never having seen it,

pale as the flesh you are born from, turned to music,
transformed into prophetic modes of feeling,
to poetry composed of vulgar snatches,

a world of Freudian slips, half-conscious puns,
longing, desire: long stockinged legs, a bra strap
struggling to be hooked, and something boiling

which you will wake to in a wasted Europe
in sixty years of endless repercussions,
millennial voodoos, chanted, domed and harried

by chorusmasters, visionaries, demons.
The clock ticks on. You don your satin slippers,
and step out into night under the planets.

*

31

Close up on the city and the clock,
the shadow stretching out along the street,
the milkbottles, the rumpled sheets, a pot
of coffee like an animal on heat...

A pencil sharpener, a barrel organ,
a woman hanging sheets out on the sill,
lovers emerging from a yellow cab,
top hats, high heels, a kiss to hold time still...

If time could be held so, a film might do it,
one we can freeze by pressing something small
and move like silent ghosts or zephyrs through it,
in readiness for the director's call.

Here everyone might greet us with a cat
outside the door, a cleaner with her broom.
Our covers are turned back, we lie down flat
and face the ceiling of the usual room.

*

Listener, listen. When we were children we heard
our parents breathing in their beds and knew
the world was beyond us, threatening, absurd
and strange as a white shark or cockatoo.

Don't turn away, I want to tell you something
from beyond the grave where our parents still spin
in obedience to the planets and the mainspring
of a universe that they found all too thin.

We're still in thrall to it. The chorus line
has felt its stern authority on their wages.
They goosestep, glide, continually combine
according to the dancing master's rages,

or move in human flags spread against soviet grass
when the band plays and all the stadium cheers
to watch the tiny faces grin and pass.
Where are you now? Where have you gone, my dears?

O blessed rage for order, pale Ramón...
I too am fascist when it suits me if that means
getting a line to strut or bend or fawn.
It is the roaring führer in my genes.

*

A block of flats somewhere in Central Europe. Let us say
a place we know. Six youths are strutting the courtyard,
a certain music in their bones, a certain rhythm to their strutting:
whoever they catch is going to catch it hard.
They hate the yids, the wogs, the reds, the greens,
emotionally living beyond their means.

Poor heavy boots. Poor razor blades. Poor hate
in the suburbs. The huddled masses at their prayer
of vengeance on a world they can't keep out.
Bad blood that follows the instinct of the slayer.
Their feet are dancing on a floor of skin,
a pouch to hold the alien organ in.

Not just the poor. Mechanics of coercion
will keep them well in line with what to think,
to sing from a single sheet, that one-off version
of reality inscribed in bright red ink
on rubricated days when all are good
and no lone wolves inhabit the dark wood.

*

But the tune is so jaunty, how could anything sinister
be associated with its upbeat drive? Here are a group
of black clad dancers, preceded by their shadows,

swarming across the stairs, filling the ballroom
with a metallic tapping, like a demented army
that knows it is a voice out of the shadows.

There's something beautiful in this, in all those limbs
moving in sensual unison, such lovely girls
in rude health and those vigorous stompers

in full seductive gear, a nightride sex
of yielding, thrust, submission, flowing round
in milky pools among voluptuous pillows,

so let me tell you, I too am seduced.
My heart breaks at this fragile dream of lust,
at being whirled away by satin dancers.

*

What is this ridiculous stomping across the ballroom of the heart?
Why are the black clad dancers swarming up glittering stairs?
What does it mean to have the world reach for you in the flower
of your beauty
when it reaches for you only to draw you away
into its own ambivalent heart like a sacrificial trophy?
That single brilliant moment, when a man knows the name of his
shadow,
the moment when bodies tremble at the verge of recognition,
of terror, desire, brutality, loss and dependence?

And as the crowd of dancers presses forward, when Dick Powell
presses his face to the glass, the voluptuous doors open
to the narrow impossible balcony where the dreamer has fled in
her panic,
the beautiful Gloria Stuart, and there we are with her, falling for
ever
into the one fulfilment, the only fulfilment on offer,

and there fall the buildings, and there fall the Jews and the gypsies,
barometers falling, falling stock values, falling lost lovers,
and something in you too, dear listener, is falling
half pleased with the pleasure, with the voice in the tunnel
that is even now falling away from you, vanishing into darkness.

*

We're watching this, you and I, from just above
the camera's shoulder and know it's only 1935.
Dick Powell is dead and the old troupe
will never again regroup
or come to life.

A table for two
A lady divine
A rhapsody blue
A bottle of wine

How low we are now. The sacrificial lovers
high above us, all flesh and all desire
and confidence, like you or I,
who cannot reach as high
but are on fire.

Then you'll listen to a siren song
Come and travel along!

COME AND DANCE
My sweetie may not let me
COME AND DANCE
Why dontcha come and get me.

*

The moment of surrender: the moment the shadow
first looms on the walls of the dance-floor, the shadow itself
        foreshadowed
by a remote thunder of feet. And something breaks at the moment
        of appearance,
something beautiful by virtue of being true to the movement
of a child's imagination, where even memory is imagined as the
        panicky noise
you make when your mother stops in the doorway or the wolf
        stops in a window.

I cannot quite manage clear articulation
of its power. It is there in the sound of a military band
in the distance, in its booming melancholy cheerfulness,
or the surge of delight when a goal is scored in a stadium,
the darkness and light of it as well as the consequence,
when the world is most edgewise, most haunted, most dreamlike.

And you know that somewhere a beating is being administered,
that a small group somewhere is busily brewing resentments
whose smell blossoms throughout the entire tenement,
and you strive to understand it as music swells past you,
knowing the danger is pitched to the perfect symbol
of a people dreaming itself into a body
that marches towards its own coda.

So ends the dream of the director Busby Berkeley
coming to you out of the depths of nineteen thirty-five,
the chorus still bent on its victim, the balcony open
and the sleeper falling headlong into life.

*

This is the girl who dreamt it all.
Blame her for beauty.
Pride goeth before a fall,
before the call of duty.

This is the girl who went to sleep
while the world was working,
this is the building tall and steep
where love and lust go lurking.

This is the band and this the stage,
this the only table.
These are the dancers in their rage
and this the Tower of Babel.

The great glass door is open wide,
the city in its glory
waits like an open mouth outside
the eleven hundredth storey.

The girl will wake up in her bed,
the clock will shudder on
with all the townscape in its head
and every dancer gone.

Glass

1

This morning I could swear we were made of glass –
tight nervous shards. Our hearts
echo in our mouths – even this desk feels brittle.
Bright clouds scuttle, smeared against the window;
men are being blown to pieces in
the doorways of villages. Women are crying
over the disgusting corpses that were children.

Powdered glass is falling through the doorway.

We are thin and bend in the heat:
slabbed in yellow light our fingers are crystal twigs
shattering over open mouths.

2

Twin asterisks of milk. An
explosion of doors in the quiet house
rouses a sleeping force to pout
under the doors of our bedroom.
Motorcycles are sick outside;
houses and dynamos turn, incendiary.

The sleek bombs wait underground
holding hands for comfort. Under
the stairs spiders are singing songs
with perfect composure.

In the pale sea-egg, all the clocks
of the world break their frail shells
and we come up fresh, smelling
of daisies, feet skyward, heads
under turf, our lips
still joined.

Father in America

When father went off to America
he wore a white suit. Later he shaved his head.
Our ancient town burned white throughout the summer
and white flowers blossomed in the cemetery –
the flowers of course remain though he is dead.

It was everybody's most idyllic picture –
white suits against pale brick or amber corn,
and gentlemen and ladies in such posture
with parasols and petticoats in pastoral
benevolence before his head was shorn.

I fear shorn heads – I touch my own skull now
and feel skin pimpling in between the roots,
with father's skull beneath. I feel it grow
progressively more bulbous under mine,
his brain is still developing new shoots.

I feel, but know that feeling isn't knowledge.
The glass distorts in the amusement park,
your skirt blows high, you cross a swaying bridge,
you hear a scream, you stand before the mirror
and face your masters in the gathering dark.

I wish this train were going elsewhere but
a wish is powerless. The skulls appear,
one on top of another. The doors are shut,
and I'd be lying if the truth were told
on picture postcards, wishing you were here.

A Card Skull in Atlantis

The *Atlantis Paper Co.* to be precise –
purveyors of artists' materials from their warehouse
in Garnet Street, a stone's throw from the river,
vendors of paint, small bottles, aerosols,
but paper chiefly – cream, pale oatmeal, speckled,
translucent, edges stiffly cut or deckled.

A pirouette of spectacular bones blew softly
in the draught of the door. You could construct
the skeleton by cutting and glueing together
the pages of a book with delicate labels:
the thing required patience to collate,
life-sized at last, if rather underweight.

There is a crystal skull, I do believe,
in the British Museum, more articulate,
more valuable perhaps, but card will do;
it grins among the sketchbooks with its patent,
its ethmoid, larmical and zygomatic,
it could even whisper something politic

of skulls like paper, piled high in ditches,
two sets of grandparents, an uncle or two,
of cousins boarding trains, securely labelled,
and people watching one another from windows.
Under the eyes their bones flare for a minute,
collapse to powder on a distant planet,

subside and sink, and form a kind of silt,
washed down by rivers, drifting among boots
and waste from sewers, sticking to dead branches,
caught by the ebb tide sun along the bank,
sucked finally to sea in salt-sour smells,
and settling dumbly among rocks and bells.

Ghost Train

Is it an illusion? It must be. Cesare
Pavese, sitting on a train, in a third-class
Carriage, alone with a woman who smokes.
He is too embarrassed to smile or make a pass
Among those empty seats that other women
Have at times vacated. It is history,
And the long train croaks
And shudders, smelling of upholstery,
Remaining empty, no place for encounters.

Public transport has been stitching together
The unfinished business of old Europe.
Believing in ghost buses that fail to stop
When requested, that appear only in foul weather,
Inhabitants of inner cities glamorise
Familiar places where the traffic chunters
Like some vigilant but dull
Official, an Argus with myopic eyes
Who cannot watch over his human cattle.
The ghost buses are empty, driverless.
They come upon one suddenly, with a noise
Of thunder and faint bells, their progress
Unsteady, vast overgrown toys
That have run away, and found this special route,
These special streets. Now someone tells a story
Of those who have managed the trick of boarding
By somehow leaping on, getting a foot
On the platform and grasping the ghost bar. According
To him their fate is terrible, a gory
Compound of brown wire, a cross between
A prison and a farmyard, shitty, poisonous.

Such buses and such trains keep rolling on.
Infected landscapes watch them, half asleep
And, perversely amorous,
They listen for flirtations in the spin
Of the wheel or the hiss of the smoke.

Now Cesare Pavese will not keep
Appointments, nor at this time of night
Is it possible to stay awake
And see the stations sweeping out of sight.

Meeting, 1944
(L.S. and M.S.)

I opened the front door and stood
lost in admiration of
a girl holding a paper box,
and that is how I fell in love.

I've come, she said, *to bring you this,*
some work from the photographer –
or rather it's for a Miss D...
Would you pass it on to her?

She's my sister, but she's out.
You must wait for her inside.
I'm expecting her right now.
Come in. I held the front door wide.

We talked a little of the war,
of what I did and what she earned;
a few minutes it was, no more,
before my sister had returned.

You're going? Well, I'm off out too.
And so we rose from our two chairs.
I'll be back shortly, Lily dear.
Shall I see you down the stairs?

That's all there is. We met again
until they took the Jews away.
I won't be long. I'll see you soon.
Write often. What else could we say?

I think they were such simple times
we died among simplicities,
and all that chaos seemed to prove
was what a simple world it is

that lets in someone at the door
and sees a pair of lives go down
high hollow stairs into the rain
that's falling gently on the town.

42

METRO

'What should they do there but desire'
DEREK MAHON

1 *At my aunt's*

My aunt was sitting in the dark, alone,
Half sleeping, when I crept into her lap.
The smell of old women now creeps over me,
An insect friction against bone
And spittle, and an ironed dress
Smoother than shells gathered by the sea,
A tongue between her teeth like a scrap
Of cloth, and an eye of misted glass,
Her spectacles with the image of a lit room
Beyond the double doors, beyond the swing
Between the doors, and my head in her bosom
At rest on soft flesh and hard corsetry,
And in that darkness a tired and perfumed smiling.

*

Across the city darkened rooms are breeding
Ghosts of elderly women, nodding off
Over the books their grandchildren are reading,
Or magazines or bibles or buttons to be sewn,
With letters, patterns, recipes, advice.
Some of them might have the radio on,
Like her, my aunt, who will remain alone
Within that room in which I visit her,
Ascending to her skin, which is rough
About the mouth, with hard nodules, like rice,
(Her face glows like a lantern) and she says,
There is a God, the God of the Jews, of Moses and Elias,
But this is not the time to speak of him.

*

And here my aunt is happy, and her sister,
Both happy in their roles. And the child
Is happy in the reading of a tale
That ends in triumph over the wild
Succubi of his imagination:
The dwarfish furies of the forest, the lank
Raincoated ghosts who pester
The living daylights out of night,
The stepmothers who live beyond the pale.
The city waits like an armchair. A slight
Woman sits there, watching, as the evenings shrink
About her, and the city opens its arms
And welcomes her to its administration.

*

There are certain places healthy to have lived in:
Certain streets, hard cores of pleasure:
Their doorways are ripe fruit, stay soft and open,
Exhaling a fragrance of drains or tobacco,
Others are more proper, starched and sun-eaten,
Doorways where things happen
In a particularly fortunate way, which echo
To words of parting, or thrill to an exact measure
Recollected in the pleat of an arch;
Doorways which see military bands march
Across a square on a blazing hot afternoon,
Or catch a particular angle of the moon.
There are places to be happy in if only you can find them.

*

The Metro provides a cheap unending ride
If you switch trains below the city.
There is a whole war to be fought out under
The pavements; I can hear the faint thunder
Of artillery in Vörösmarty Square:
The cobbles shake, move gently from side to side
With microscopic accuracy, and ice creams
Wobble in their goblets. The cavity
Beneath the streets is filled with the blare
Of surface traffic. The city is all dreams
And talk, and rumours of talk. The place below
Is treacherous. You don't know
Who your friends are, who you are yourself.

*

It is everything that is past, the hidden half,
A subcutaneous universe in which
Our fate is to be the dramatis personae
Of geographers who place us more precisely
Than we can ourselves. I place a woman
On a train and pack her off to Ravensbruck:
I send out a troop of soldiers to summon
The Jews of this fair city.
                      Off she goes,
Repeating her unknown journey, and I must look
To gauge the distances between us nicely.
I see a voice, the greyest of grey shadows.
Lead me, psychopompos, through my found
City, down into the Underground.

*

2 Undersongs

I love the city, the way it eats you up
And melts you into walls along with stone
And stucco till your voice assumes a tone
As crinkled, crenellated, creviced as itself,
And you can recognise it in a shop
Like something heard through windows. Human forms,
Detail and allegory: the twelve
Months of the year, the forces of nature, or
A frieze of leaves and angels where the worms
Have eaten away the substance of a voussoir
Above a flaking open door,
A spray of lace or foam, a mouchoir
In plaster flung at the late empire.

*

The empire underground: the tunnelling
Begins. The earth gives up her worms and shards,
Old coins, components, ordnance, bone and glass,
Nails, muscle, hair, flesh, shrivelled bits of string,
Shoe leather, buttons, jewels, instruments.
And out of these come voices, words,
Stenches and scents,
And finally desire, pulled like a tooth.
It's that or constancy that leads us down
To find a history which feels like truth.
The windows cannot speak because we pass
Before them all too often but the bricks know
What they stand on. There is no town below,

*

It's only bits and pieces, as above.
You have to watch your language though: the words
Are muddy, full of unintended puns
And nervy humour. Waking afterwards
You feel soiled and dirty, the one you chased
Has vanished, shown a clean pair of heels.
The Metro thunders through like heavy guns
To shake the waking streets. They are effaced,
And reconstructed, effaced again.
Now where are you, psychopompos?
Who'll pick up your thread or catch your train,
Who'll follow you and bear your mouldered cross
Through tunnels tight as fingers in a glove?

*

Desire again, the undersong. The lost
Children feel it in their sleep,
And turn uneasily to the wall through which
Symbols pass and cool their blood like ghosts.
My mother's family has passed through it,
Not one remains, and she is half way through.
Her brother disappears, the glove has closed
About him somewhere and dropped him in the ditch
Among the rest. The ditch becomes a pit,
The pit a symbol, the symbol a desire,
And this desire's the thread. The tunnels creep
Under the skin, the trains with their crew
Of passengers can glide through unopposed.

*

Their voices are not heard but seen, are moving
Lips and tongues. They're well behaved and quiet.
To give voice is to lip read, to construe
The contortions of a mouth, to place the living
Where the dead are, your money where their mouth is.
The body longs for touch: no words are spoken,
But sentences break up, are made new
Into fictions which will occupy the city
Like a foreign army. Their all too tangible bodies
Litter up the place, these men and women
Travelling. Her voice is underground.
Her poetry (unseen and without sound)
Lies not in pity but in clarity.

*

The Metro runs along to City Park,
That is a fact, and all along the line
The shivering persists beneath your feet.
The same with facts. It is a chance remark
That lingers in the tunnels, is embedded
In pavements, under skin or in the grain
Of your bench. She steps in, finds a seat
And is whisked off to meet my father in
A flat in Rózsa Street. His heavy-lidded
Eye remembers, re-encounters. The street
Of the rose. The rest is not my business,
But a picture in a frame. Under the skin
She wears another skin, another dress.

*

3 *Portraits*

At fourteen she went skating on the river
And caught a cold. *The boys would come from far*
To sing outside my window, there were many –
Because I was attractive and vivacious.
The cold developed into rheumatic fever,
Thrombosis followed. Then would follow a litany
Of lost relations, lost names, and the brother
Who failed to love her, who was beautiful.
The town was Cluj, then known as Kolozsvár,
The district Transylvania. From this
Follows the following, expand the cool
Shadows of biography and synopsis.
Even now I know little about my mother.

*

From this and something more, the skeleton
Of something – body, city, staircase, wall –
Which feels impressive, is part visible;
From this follow internment and arrest,
The family hatreds and the fierce ungracious
Vendettas of my childhood, and the fiction
Of history which makes up Budapest
And what one thinks of as oneself, that one
Who thinks he sees, who wears both belt and braces
In photographs, an infant contradiction,
A narrator, himself of morbid interest,
Whose scented aunt and God have settled down,
Whose eyes shut windows in the city's face,

*

A peculiar little old man of a boy,
A kind of dwarf, benevolently wise
And puzzled, deep voiced, comical almost.
He kneels under a table, his bare bottom
Sticking in the air, a bendy toy.
He swings between the doorway, opens his eyes
And thinks he sees the faint trace of a ghost
Among the coats left hanging on the hook,
Touches the piano, examines the vast stove
Which dominates the corner of the room,
Deploys his troops on battlefields of blankets,
And colonises every possible alcove
Of his world with a vague unfocused look.

*

The early fifties: Uncle Joe's broad grin
Extends benevolently across the wall.
The boy wears a Young Drummers uniform
(A blue tie with a toggle), shakes the hand
Of dignitaries at some parade. He is thin
And pinlike, almost cavernous. The school
Is pleased. He's learning to perform.
She works and he works. She checks his work for him
And terrifies him into excellence.
He has a line of stars in his book. They're hers.
He watches her pupils contract and expand.
Uncle Joe's moustache will shelter them.
This is the era of benevolence.

*

Her likenesses are caught on film. Her hair
Has flared into a dark corona, black beams
Of sunlight, thick, now piled high, now falling.
It hides her face. She stands on the ramparts
Of the Bastion, her teeth gleam.
Her finger can bend backwards in a curve
That is quite frightening. She deploys her arts
Of fascination as he does his troops.
She sits down on a chair,
Invites him to her lap. He will deserve
Her attentions. He listens to her calling.
His father enters and pulls him through the snow.
She smokes a cigarette and parts her lips.

*

He's easily frightened; when she lashes round
In a monumental fury he keeps her sting
In the bottom drawer. It is his occupation
To bring it out at night and scare himself.
For a long time he can sit and watch her working,
And feel her warmth, and listen to the sound
Of her breathing. It gives him an odd sensation
Of belonging/not belonging, half and half.
This half and half will always seem like truth
(I too can see him only with one eye).
He'll keep her face and others in the drawer,
With her own photographs, her frozen youth,
Her unsent letters, his unwritten reply.

*

4 *Flying backwards*

The accident of being who one is.
The accident of being in a place
At one time not another. It is not grace
Of form, but grace of accident that gives
A building power, and lends the body strength,
The necessary structure to survive.
The tattered dress of fortune parodies
Our specious dignity. It makes us eat
Our words, as I eat hers, takes breadth and length
And swallows them whole. It is the street
Of Roses. It is the beautiful brother.
The things that might smell sweet by any other
Name we give, or recall by accident.

*

I have her brother's face – a studio piece
Of *circa* '29, and then again
Some two years later, hair cropped tight about
His delicate skull. She stands beside him, pouts
And stares, waiting for him to release
Her trapped hand. Photography, her trade,
Is this security, this collateral:
My fiction turns to sepia in its presence,
All subterfuge is instantly displayed
For what it is, a brief ingenious pattern.
And he cared so little for me if at all.
I tried to find him later but in vain.
My words for what she meant, in a general sense.

*

The uncle with the chocolate factory,
The uncle who was magistrate,
The father who travelled to the States
And worked as a labourer. The middle-class
Jews of Kolozsvár are the lost history
Of which she hardly spoke. Mother's bob
Is a fashionable frame for her neat face,
Which the edges of the photograph reframe.
They bind the sepia, prevent it spilling
Across the desk, hold names
At an aesthetic distance, where, by willing,
We can work them into fictions and animate
The past, which remains forever another place.

*

But it does spill over. It is what we are
And what we see and time and again forget.
It's there in walls, in Uncle Joe's moustache
Which is the wall. The other place is here
And grows moustaches, breasts, Edwardian collars,
Wears miniskirts and co-respondent shoes.
Whatever preserves the late imperial texture
Of before, that keeps the pattern true
And cynical, expresses its regret
In the rhetoric of faded architecture,
The blatant half truth / half light of a picture,
A vulgar hybrid of fleeting, local colour
Where only light is faithfully reproduced.
The rest is reconstruction and conjecture.

*

The rest is data such as: *At the hour*
When the Germans entered Budapest we were
Sitting in the Astoria, or *The man*
Who called for us wore glasses. Or *She used*
A certain colour lipstick...Such power
As we retain resides in these. I build her
In Meccano. Here's the skeleton.
The bare bones of the story are reduced
To ashes and a name in Golders Green,
Behind the Hippodrome, behind the station.
Recovered from thrombosis, at eighteen
She left for Budapest, an invitation
In her handbag (possibly her pocket).

*

She worked as a photographer. The war had started
But you'd hardly know it. She met my father late,
When he returned from camp in Proskyrov.
It was February, 1944.
Next month the Germans entered Budapest
And he was recalled to unit. The date,
Nineteenth of March. Facts, bare bones, the rest
Are silences. A 'safe house' in August
With father's family two floors above.
September, October, the Arrow Cross, the raid.
Her feet are clattering in the gallery,
His family are hiding or departed
And only she remains to be betrayed.

*

5 *Betrayals*

Betrayed? She felt and thought she was. But who
Betrayed her (if it was betrayal) and how?
Betrayal by omission was the way,
Betrayal by those she trusted. Down below,
The soldiers in the yard, the quasi-military.
They called her down. It was a minute's work.
But why was she out on the gallery
When it was far more sensible to hide?
And why did no one tell her? Who were they
Who should have done so? Why did they shirk
Their human duty? The wound was always fresh:
Even at fifty-one, the year she died,
It bored and tunnelled deep into her flesh,

*

Katona József Street. The Swedish house.
My father's family came from the North,
Moravia and Bohemia, tailors, painters,
Vendors of musical instruments, a broker,
And father's father was a shoemaker.
How much is all this information worth?
The list is endless and monotonous,
Their season's over, summers, autumns, winters:
Few made the final spring of '45.
My father had been brought up by the aunts
Who coddled me in my turn. To survive
Was an achievement, but my grandparents
Were under-achievers all of them, bar one.

*

My father's mother. Large-eyed, beaky-nosed.
We must have met but I've no recollection,
Except of something owl-like, something scented.
Her absence gave her little enough protection
From mother's fury. The matter was closed,
No letters exchanged. In '56 she went
To Argentina, wrote, sent messages,
But his replies were censored or forbidden.
Her case was settled. Sometimes she sent me presents,
Pale useless things, the kind my mother resented
And fanned her hatred for her. It was the hidden
Secret of my childhood, what she'd done.
Even now I don't know what the truth is.

*

My aunts (or great-aunts to be precise)
Brought father up. His home was there. The owl
Had farmed him out. When evidence
Was weighed at home this counted much against her
And nobody replied in her defence.
Numerus clausus, numerus nullus: twice
Father was hit by laws against the Jews,
His education stopped, he worked in knit-wear,
Was twice promoted then forced out. A friend
Advised him, trained him, offered him a place
He couldn't decently refuse:
Apprentice plumber, master of the bowl.
For both of them it was an hour of grace.

*

Inevitably, labour camps. How many
Perished here: the artists, writers,
Musicians, plumbers, brothers? Escapades,
Adventures, tragedies, the company
Reduced, disbanded then recalled.
The dark-eyed girl in February, back home.
Road building, retreat, escape. The waters
Close about my grandfather and fold
Over him in Auschwitz. Brief episodes
Of dire intensity, each trivial sum
A fortune lost. The dark-eyed girl moves in
With father's mother, sister, baby niece.
It's lists and rosters, jigsaws piece by piece.

*

They fall together, stand and fall together.
The day the soldiers came she was alone
And heard them shouting. On another floor
The female threesome. She looks for them. The door
Is open. She calls their names, the mother,
Sister, niece. They do not answer. Where have they gone?
Where are they hiding? Nothing. Not a sound.
She wanders out, is spotted. It is fear:
Fear of discovery, fear of strangers. It's done.
They have not answered. Someone shouts, Come down!
And who is it pretended not to hear?
The rough voice rises. I speak for another
And buy my ticket for the underground.

*

6 *In Her Voice*

Like a girl listening behind
A membrane for a footfall or the knock
On a door, the rattling of the blinds
In a secret room of her head, I unlock
My eyelids pressed
Against a darkened window in a house
Whose eyes are asleep,
And quietly get undressed.
I have a thousand eyes to guard my neatness
Against the gods of lust, who quaintly creep
To music as they blind me and I wake
To hear the scuttling of a mouse
Here on the fourth floor at one o'clock.

*

I was on the fourth floor when the yard
Filled with uniforms and we were called
To order, and I ran into the flat we shared,
The old woman, her daughter and the child,
And all was empty. I whispered their names
But they did not answer to their lasting shame.
They should have answered me out of the pit,
Like any prompter from his own hell-hole,
But they closed their mouths to my pitiful dole
So I went down and here's the end of it.
Those men have strolled at ease about our yard
But God will grant them their reward
And punish them according to their lot.

*

They took me in their wagon, up the street
I used to walk, with all its empty faces
Staring from the coigns and pediments.
Great figures started from the roof in tents
Of stone and tiling, forgetting the discreet
Darkness of their long discolouration,
And tiny figures flitted by the bases
Of the portico of the academy.
My mind showed little sign of occupation:
All life was going on outside, upheld
By the conventions of the weather,
My tenants were expelled
To railway stations where we lost each other.

*

They put me on a train, east, west or south
And we rode off in our different directions,
Myself, my body and my heart. My eyes
Were saying something to my open mouth
Which had remained open in surprise
And every passenger had his own questions:
My nose asked, what's the smell?
My fingers wondered at the touch of cold,
My hair was busy interrogating the wind.
We were all agog to know the world at last
As it knew itself but never before had told
Anyone. Nor did I mind
Whether this was heaven, earth or hell,

*

As long as we were moving in the air,
As long as the city barked its orders out
Through doorways I imagined everywhere
And heard the porters shout
Behind closed eyes and behind the narrow wall
Of my most valued multi-storeyed skull.
But they told me no great truth or if they did
I have forgotten it. It was long ago
And I have doubts whether such a truth
Exists at all, as something we might know
Or understand. I have my hatred
Which is proof that something happened in my youth,
And the house itself has not yet been blown down,

*

My body is still standing. The wind blows through it
Like a language of which not a word
Is what it seems, and yet it survives.
The train is rushing past the fields and woods
Of all that was. The words renew it,
Rephrase its truths and falsehoods.
Behind the thinnest of walls a city thrives,
The empty buildings, the unfurnished,
Whose history remains unfinished.
    I rush out to the gallery, alone
And watch the soldiers massing underneath,
My brothers all, their justice bone for bone,
Their eyes are my eyes, their teeth are my teeth.

*

7 *What should they do there but desire*

Disorientation, loss: the doors that close
Just when you think that you have gained your entrance.
A glimpse of hallway, hat-rack, mirror, more doors.
Beyond the doors and on the left perhaps
A window giving on to a neat yard
With trees and flowers. Straight ahead of you
A lift-cage dressed in iron broderie,
A smell of coffee brewing, an envelope
Slit like a wound, the darker recesses
Of sitting rooms, momentarily opened.
What troubles me is the uncertainty:
Is this really a valuable darkness,
Or am I part of the darkness that's locked out?

*

The wind is scrabbling at the glass – perhaps
The trees are wanting to be let in.
The branches say nothing
Expressing only an incoherent thirst
For music, a music so violent and awful
That it can only leave them waving their arms.
Imagine the cellos sprouting dark green tongues
And moaning softly of their lot; their past
Of growing, cutting, hewing, shaping
To this one point of supreme helplessness.
What's eating them? And yet it's good to be eaten,
To become the food of passion and to feel
The stomach rise in suicidal independence.

*

The wind stands in high places and looks down
And comes out at your arsehole and your mouth.
I do not speak now as a lady should,
Not even as a woman, but of parts,
The one dissociated from the other.
When I think of you I only see your head,
Sometimes a hand. The wind runs through your fingers
And cools the blood to a blue stream of air,
And when I hear it scrabbling at the glass
I'm filled with pride and understand the light
That leaps inside me and across the table
To reach out for some part, a head or hand
Or thigh or foot or armpit, something of you...

*

Some years ago I met a man by chance
In a foreign street. I had not seen him since
The time when I last saw my brother
Of whom I carry about this sepia
(I seem to be my brother's only keeper)
Which is paler than he was. I blame the weather
For his fading and our having grown estranged.
He was handsomer than any man I knew,
As handsome as a woman could desire.
*   There was a policeman once who doffed his cap*
And showed how in the lining he arranged
His family in tiers of small brown snaps.

Photography, I need you. Freeze me too.

*

Even here there are shadows of places: serene,
Impassive, idiotic, undemanding,
Without bitterness or rancour.
We are travelling in darkness, standing
On each other's feet but at one remove.
The door of the wagon rattles a pale music.
An elderly man is sick in the straw.
A child clings to my thigh. Two grown men kick
Each other in a fury, or try to gnaw
A third man's head. What do these things prove?

It is the peculiar happiness of buildings
To be witnesses. Here are the stones and mouldings,
The molten forms of clinker.

*

Dear brother, I have talked to everyone
But no one knows you. I am sitting in
A wooden hut, rather like a kennel.
You're well away from here. A woman kicks us
As she passes. I do not trust the women.
The men we're used to, they are what they are,
The usual sheep, but I'm a woman and
I know that pitch of the heart,
Am living in it. Who are they paying back?
Their elder brothers? Wherever you are
This non-existent paper will locate you,
In the angle of the wood, the nursery,
Or up the cherry tree with its sticky black cherries.

*

8 *Stopping train*

Here's Ravensbruck. I stop dead at the gate,
Aware I cannot reach you through the wire.
I cannot send you poems or messages,
No wreath of words arranged across blank pages,
No art that thrives on distance and desire,
But can't cope with fulfilment, that writes white
When happiness breaks out, that lights a taper
On a frozen lawn and bounces off the stones
Of hard luck. The dead have no use for art.
You might as well bring on the tongs and bones
As chamber music (Schubert's great quintet).
Not all the white ink in the world can set
Their coming through, their verses on black paper.

*

And if I bring you here and push you in
It's only because I know you once came out.
You cross the black bridge thus. *Ich bin allein,*
Ich stell die Aschenblume ins Glass voll
Reifer Schwärze, deep into your mouth.
And if I attribute to you desire
It is to replace what was voluptuous
In bodies full of warmth, *das aschenes Haar*
Which is also mine. I wait outside your school
Of hard correction, mouthing words too soft
To bear a lasting mark, a feminine tongue
In my head. I float on my own craft,
And try to write the half dead a live song.

*

Dead grandfathers, dead grandmother, dead uncles.
Item: to my children, All the aunts
Their grandparents can muster, this bequest
To be taken by them for granted. Tender plants
Turn vast familial trees in paradise,
Which is nothing else but superfluity,
Where every woman has an extra breast,
And every generation's spoiled for choice.
A balloon floated past our window and almost
Touched the bricks. Small green leaves covered
The trees. So wrote one Nelly Toll in Lwow.
Superfluous in base things, we are lost
In distant towns whose names sound much like Love.

*

See, in this drawing a girl is making Lwow.
Her mother and she are playing dominoes,
The sunflowers are growing in the shadows.
Small green leaves cover the trees. Above,
A balloon floats past the window. *I visited*
The children on paper. Paper of deep black
Is lightened by her painting. Even the dead
March cheerly in their prison, and look back
On paradise, and know that God is Lwow.
Ich stell die Aschenblume ins Glas voll
Reifer Schwärze. The camp choir sings a mass,
The camp dogs chew their bones. And in the glass
A brilliant ash-grey flower for Nelly Toll.

*

She tolls me back to the bleak scene before
The entrance. The women march to the factory.
Their wooden shoes are tottering on the ice;
It sounds like someone knocking at the door.
Thirty years on the knocking hasn't stopped,
But now your heart wears out its battery,
Is running down, its tick-tock, less precise,
Is more like memory, which soon is lost
And drifts above the garden in fine dust.
Like Lili Marlene I wait outside the gate,
A lamplit watchdog expecting no returns.
Imagine my surprise when you walk out.
The crematorium waits, the oven burns.

*

This is our lucky day, like every day.
The white ink settles on the page like snow.
The sunflowers are growing in the shadow.
The crows are circling looking for dead meat.
Your hair turns into flowers streaked with grey:
I put them in a glass. The room grows warm
With soft grey flowers, responds with its own heat.
The pillows, blankets, curtains are in bloom
And open into grey. The grey flies swarm
About the lamp. This is our mortal room.
A train is arriving at an empty station.
A voice is speaking, but it isn't mine.
The passengers are spilled across the line.

*

9 *Fraternal Greetings*

Beauty and terror, just enough to bear:
The Rilkean brother, a little lower than
The lowest angel whose indifference
Is murderous to those who marvel at him
And expect him to return love like a man.
Disdain is an improvement on despair,
And hatred perhaps a kind of confidence
Which can be shared like intimacy,
Unexplained antipathy or dim
Persistent loathing. No analysis
Avoids abstraction. For some there is no physic
Or improvement. When instructed to kiss
His baby sister my uncle was violently sick.

*

And so there's guilt, guilt and indifference:
He in his turn became idealised
As all disdainful gods are. That is why
They are gods. And this was no pretence:
He could be human, true, but not to her.
She called him 'freedom fighter', 'partisan'
Once she had lost him. For a god to die
Is only to gain in potency, to rise
A few clouds higher – and it might have been all true
Although I heard he was a prisoner
And laboured, like my father, like a man,
And then might have been shot, aged twenty-two
Somewhere in Slovakia perhaps.

*

Perhaps. And yet he simply disappeared.
Tall forehead, dark hair, full and sensuous mouth,
Intense, intelligent. But to be sick
At touching her? Are gods sick at our touch?
It's possible of course. The bright one's beard
Is sensitive. It bristles at our youth
And emptiness. To him, we stink of pitch,
Are lymph and chyle and hatred. When we raise
Our holocausts to him he looks away.
He's not pleased by the smoke of sacrifice,
Or tawdry festivals or holy days,
Is tired of them. The gods have seen so much
Of fire they begin to turn to ice.

*

It's not that they mind the flattery: the smell
Is what offends them and they cannot help it.
So he's a god too, and whatever pit
His murderers interred him in he rose
And faded, entered other realms like hell
Or heaven. And she in her hell yearned
For his beauty and affection all the more.
Desire and pain. Around her bodies burned
In their own fevers or behind the door
That was always round the corner. I propose
A yard, a hut, a fence, a row of beds
And shins and shanks and ribs and collarbones,
And one familiar among shaven heads.

*

Those burning babes, visions of Christmas day,
The small photographers, provincial towns,
Perversities, distortions. They move down
The escalator, spread along the platform.
The train arrives and takes them. More keep coming.
Each face desires another. They pray
With a look, communicate by grimacing.
Each one of them is in some uniform
Of obsolescent dullness. Each bears a name
On the collar or the sleeve. Their names are numbers.
Above their mouths a single flickering flame
Sustains their spirit, and like spirit, it burns
And dances and reduces them to cinders.

*

Dear brother, I have talked...the voice is distant
As the past it conjures, as the little boy
Under the table...*but no one knows you.* To know
Is not to see or understand. The grey
Fly hovers at the curtain without knowing
That any particular thing is so
Or otherwise, but his drone remains insistent.
The walls keep mouthing at us with their doorways,
The trains keep coming and going.
The ghosts must pass through the walls alone,
Take on the character of stone,
Seek out the angle of the wood, the nursery,
Climb up the cherry tree with its sticky black cherries...

*

10 *The little time machine*

Burnt offerings: a little bonfire shivers
At the far end of the street, all rags and card
And insignificance. A wheelbarrow
Is propped like an old man kissing the pavement,
A stiff frock coat, the mud on the wheel his beard.
The flames leap and fall in rapid rivers
Of light, a confusion of elements.
I see small fires along the narrow
Passages between main thoroughfares.
The heart, the eyes and passions maintain
Their vigilance. The holocaust goes up
In smoke. Somewhere a soldier prepares
To set fire to fine details on a street map.

*

The map is always burning. Its consumption
Is conspicuous enough, imagined cities
Of fugitive colour, changing light on tiles,
Faces at windows, hands at doorways, feet
On trams and buses, clothes in smelly piles
In empty hallways, the sonorities
Of gossip and greeting. My friends and I meet
At restaurants, complaining of hard times
In the benevolence of an August night
That smiles on our children. We are an exception
To the rules of sleep. Our children will sleep light.
After the fireworks we tell old jokes
And pay our debt to history with rhymes.

*

The city dreams an island. It has always
Been here, stacked on its mound of days,
Lapped by cold sea, pickled and saline,
Wearing, breaking off. Hard water furs
The kettles, houses fall, rejig the shoreline,
Everything is continually in friction
With the wind off the sea. The women with scarves,
The men pottering in sheds, seek protection
In distance, the insularity of it all.
Sad, great, shaggy country. The soldier hears,
Takes aim and fires but misses. Foreign flotsam
Adheres to the feet of piers by decaying wharves.
The ferries shuttle. Waves crack on the wall.

*

The crack of a gate. Time opens backward to
A heap of pebbles suspiciously like bodies.
The wind whistles through trains whose nightmare crew
Of passengers have fallen quiet, stopped
Their grimacing and squealing and have dropped
Where they stood, dropped off to sleep at last
In broken postures, parodies
Of grace, recumbency and carelessness.
It is only by imagining the trains
That I can enter the gate, walk across the field,
And wait for the signals to announce the express
Europa. Its carriages are sealed,
The wheels go rattling over broken chains.

*

Too long rejected, we meet up in the street
Below a lamp post, yellowed as old papers.
What news? we ask each other. Our faces
Are the cut-out shapes of childhood, full of creases
And torn edges, smudged and circled
In soft chalks. We've brought along with us
Giraffes and elephants in a discreet
Procession, with dolls and packs of cards, and pieces
Of furniture arranged in packing cases.
Nothing but dust and detritus.
This is the news, hot off the world's press.
It's late at night, you say. We are light sleepers,
I reply, our sleep is a kind of emptiness.

*

Somebody has escaped at last. Somebody gets married,
Has a child, another. Somebody remembers
Someone else or something, certain numbers,
Certain streets and faces. One is worried
By forgetfulness, another by clarity.
Someone is not sure they should be here.
  Down into the Metro, down the stair:
A drunken woman's weeping on a bench,
Another's sitting in a pool of water,
The horrible familiar stench
Of loss. A fat policeman nudges
At them. The crowd skirts round the edges
Of the frame, spreads out into the city.

*   *   *

After Attila

(a version after Attila József)

The storm arrives, a froth of black,
A dark and sullen lumbering;
Lightning snickers, cuts a track
Of light across the slumbering
Landscape, like a shot of pain
Under the scalp, and then again,
A velvet shimmering and rumbling
Sets the jasmine quietly trembling.

See, apple-blossom – the twig is snapped –
Her petals, those poor butterfly-wings,
Attempt to fly, the foolish things.

Down the gentle slope the trapped
Mobs of wild grass bend and sway
Fearing the dark has come to stay.

Their shuddering, however frail,
Is good to teach their little ones
To bear the terror of the gale;
Learn then, my dear, when trouble comes
To sing your terror soft and low
So that the very grass may know
Your voice, and think that, as you pass,
You yourself are only grass.

The Impotence of Chimneys

Silent spouters, barrels, tall comical brothers,
you have reached the age of puberty
and impotence at one and the same time.
The fire in the groin is merely smoke,
the cloud will never rain. How quickly
it disperses and your stumps go gathering
their wits for one pale archaism which
will offend no one. See, even the dead,
how apologetically they fade and blow
above the crematorium, their smoke
invisible, floating about the town
like dandelion seeds. The fat pink Popeye
forearms, the ornate iron hats, are raised
to acknowledge the old Viennese truth
that in between the one fire and the other
we can afford the gentleness of smoke,
secreting pain beneath its decent whiskers
with Lear's menagerie, his nagging cricket.

Grandfather in Green

My grandfather, the Budapest shoemaker,
    wrote plays in his spare time, and then he died.
His body became a pebble on a beach
    of softness across which swept the pale green tide.

Pale green, I think, would suit him as a tint –
    under his eye, or thinly flexed across
the hooked bridge of his nose. His sour complexion
    was cooking apples, a summary of loss,

each a pucker in the flesh. His waistcoat
    was grey as clouds, a pale green handkerchief
blossoming from the pocket. Even his tongue
    would sit in his mouth, soft and green as a leaf.

And so he returned to nature after all,
    the pale green gall within him in the shut
cavern of his stomach, and the green
    smell of gas still lingering in the hut.

Losing

We lose each other everywhere:
the children in department stores
return as parents, *fils et père*
collide by the revolving doors.

The pavements' litter, burning flakes
of bonfires, tickets and franked stamps,
the fragile image drops and breaks,
the fugitive awakes, decamps.

The carriages uncouple, trucks
return unladen, suits appear
on vacant charitable racks,
the shelves of darkened stockrooms clear,

skin lifts and peels. A cake of soap.
The human lamps, the nails, the hair,
the scrapbooks' chronicles of hope
that lose each other everywhere.

Threnody

(for Matt Simpson)

Wipe the white beard. Let it lie across his chest.
Smooth it flat and close his eyes too while you're at it.
What is history but a beard as white as this?
Gather the length gently, ribbon it and plait it.

The breath is long stopped and the words are all fading.
The air's no longer his. His was another planet –
Pluto, Jupiter – the dear one, so distant,
a spirit floating about cupboard and cabinet,

father of fathers, a well-tempered clavier,
God in the machine in the corner of the room.
Take up his name, cut it out with reverence,
and paste it on a new page of the family album.

Dry mouths and dry names, shells of dead insects,
heaps of moth-wings, beetle-shards, disinfected,
no thought of flight now or crawling, they lurk
in the annals, sad husks, untongued, undetected,

in rooms of faint darkness with the sound of ghost feet
across halls of vague carpet and trousers in a chair,
in long-distance calls and buckles in the mirror,
faces of children: thick dark hair.

A Soldier

(after Károly Escher)

A young man with two flowers in his cap
Has turned away across the platform
To move towards two women wearing headscarves.
He is the country I am leaving.

He is beautiful, a beast decked and garlanded,
He stands gently and placidly, tall, slim,
Melancholy, prepared for sacrifice,
A peasant soldier, simple as they come.

Death has half closed his eyes
Ready to devour him at a blinking.
Behind his head the blur of a wagon pulling out.
He seizes one of the women, embraces her,

Presses himself against her.
As we depart I am tempted to shout
To attract his attention. I can only guess
The occasion of his death, his tenderness.

THE COURTYARDS

At the Dressing-table Mirror

She sits at the dressing-table, pushing back her hair,
Lipstick in hand, eyes poised above the quivering stick,

Aware of someone – a boy – moving behind her, watching,
Observing the dark hair falling onto her shoulders

And trying to remove without her noticing
A thing she cannot see from the handbag on the bed:

But she has only to turn to her right to check on his movements
And the reflection that showed her now shows the boy also

And what he does beside her in that mirror, in the room
They both occupy...United for an instant

In that glance, surprised by the net in which they find
Themselves doing what their image shows them doing,

They break on the very edge of laughter, clearer for
A second in that marriage, till she leans forward to

Apply the lipstick, when her breathing mists the glass
And the boy and woman are parted. But still, many years after,

Throwing out old books or turning up a card
In her writing, or noticing a look in his daughter's eye

To arrest him at his work, he sees at once the mirror
And hears again their shared and broken laughter.

The Photographer in Winter
(i.m. M.S. 1924-1975)

> *for M.V. and O.O.*

> '*He was hurrying along with frozen hands and watering eyes*
> *when he saw her not ten metres away from him. It struck him*
> *at once that she had changed in some ill-defined way.*'
> ORWELL

You touch your skin. Still young. The wind blows waves
Of silence down the street. The traffic grows
A hood of piled snow. The city glows.
The bridges march across a frozen river
Which seems to have been stuck like that for ever.
The elderly keep slipping into graves.

Your camera is waiting in its case.
What seems and is has never been less certain –
The room is fine, but there beyond the curtain
The world can alter shape. You watch and listen.
The mirror in the corner seems to glisten
With the image of a crystalline white face.

Too many marvels. Pagodas, ziggurats;
The follies of the snow. Geometries
In miniature, the larger symmetries
Of cars, the onion domes of bollards, spires
On humble kiosks, stalactites on wires,
A vast variety of dazzling hats.

The white face in the mirror mists and moves
Obscure as ever. Waves of silence roll
Across the window. You are in control
Of one illusion as you close your eyes.
The room, at least, won't take you by surprise
And even in the dark you find your gloves.

*

Where are you going? To work? I'm watching you.
You cannot get away. I have been trained
To notice things. But all will be explained
And you will know why it is necessary
To follow you like this. In the meantime, carry
On as usual, do what you would normally do.

You catch the tram? I'll sit behind you where
You will not find me. I see your every move.
Believe me when I say you would approve
Such thoroughness and objectivity.
So this is the route you take across the city.
The tram goes rattling on. You touch your hair

Before you stand and walk off down the street.
Your hair is swinging loosely. The snow breaks
My picture up. It needs a few more takes
To get this right. Your costume is correct
Historically speaking? They will expect
Immaculate appearances, discreet

Camera angles, convincing details. Please
Co-operate with me and turn your head,
Smile vacantly as if you were not dead
But walked through parallel worlds. Now look at me
As though you really meant it. I think we could be
Good for each other. Hold it right there. Freeze.

*

You can't remember and you can't redeem
The faces altered with a loaded brush,
Faces who drift before you as you wash
The prints in faint red light, pure images
Of births and funerals and marriages.
The snow has lost them. Even when you dream

They merge confusingly. The children throw
White bombs at one another which explode
Splattering their clothes; and, across the road,
A white-haired man reveals his youthful skin.
You see the building he's been living in
And you yourself have aged. He turns to go

But leaves his face behind, a different face
With no expression but the features set.
You cannot quite remember where you met
But go on meeting. Doorways, offices.
The dream creates an odd paralysis.
He seems to move, you're frozen in your place.

Wake up, wake up. The faces disappear.
Your own must be put on. You look a mess
And draw a veil over your tiredness.
The curtains lift. Your hair must be swept back
Before the wind which gives you a loud smack
And forces out an unexploded tear.

*

Some elegance is what you crave, a touch
Of silver in the grey light of the street,
A hint of Strauss to fill the room, the beat
Of the Radetzky March, or other such
Imperial themes. Ironic music, gay,
But not unfitting in its own small way.

Exaggerations, nothing more. You climb
Eight flights of stairs, immerse yourself
In private smells. The novels on the shelf
Begin to yellow. You can measure time
In their coarse pages, in the damp, the space
Between the deadpan mirror and your face.

The mirror throws her silvered answer back.
A breath takes you away beyond the glass
Into a land of fog and rain. Hours pass
Like dim processions, tiny boats, a track
Of dirty water, and the music plays
While breath evaporates. The image stays.

The gods of gracious living pass us by.
They hear you vaguely as the marches fade
Above the humming of their motorcade.
Dear woman, train your photographic eye
On me and the dead wall where I must wait
For you to reappear, however late.

*

Hand colouring. It was a form of art,
And when you bent over your work I saw
How art could not obey a natural law,
That faces flowered and that teeth shone pale
As distant neon: memory would fail
To keep the living and the dead apart.

To be quite honest, it was creepy watching
This process of embalmment (as it seemed),
To see the smoothed-out features, the redeemed
Perfection of the unbelievable, showing
No signs of ever having lived, but glowing
Pink and white. I found it strangely touching.

And that was art, you said. The difficult.
But you were lying or just didn't know,
And even then, so many years ago,
The images had started to assume
The frozen aspect of an empty room,
Imperfect, white and granular as salt.

And now it's winter, and this dreadful weather
Is always at the very edge of spring
But cannot make or fake it. I can't bring
Another year to light. You sit alone
With all the pictures that the wind has blown
Away and art must somehow fit together.

*

This winter is not metaphorical.
The sun has broken into tiny pieces
And goes on fracturing as it releases
More and more light, which decorates the walls
With stud-medallions and hangs up crystals
On high wires, where they shudder, trip and fall

And break again. Sometimes it is water
Creeping down a window, a sharpened pen
Above the lintel, a white screen which men
Must penetrate like knives, a curious shriek
Which cuts the eye. A square of film must seek
To capture intact this wild and wholesale slaughter.

I go on taking pictures all the same.
I shoot whole rolls of film as they shoot me.
We go on clicking at the world we see
Disintegrating at our fingers' ends,
As if, by stopping time, we made amends
For all that time destroyed outside the frame.

I watch her working. Now and then I've tried
To catch her eye but found the snow had grown
A brilliance which sunlight made its own
And broke on impulse, as it breaks a train
Of thought, or breaks (it seems) a windowpane
That seems to show her on the other side.

*

What awful cold we seem to have had this year.
A winter of betrayals. Even words
Drop dead in flight, and, afterwards,
We try to sweep them up, quite uselessly.
I can hardly see a hand in front of me.
Everything is speckled. Nothing is clear.

Imagine trying to focus through this swirl
And cascade of snow. It's dark already.
Impossible to keep the picture steady
In the wind. An early evening filters in
Behind the white – my gloves are much too thin
To keep it out. I think I am a girl.

'To be alone in winter is like dying,'
She sings. Here everyone is alone. We die
Of the cold. It can be dangerous to cry
When tears freeze on your cheeks. We must have courage
And think of winter as a happy marriage,
The kiss of snow, the wind's contented sighing.

We must have courage till the spring regains
Her confidence. Courage is everything.
I load the camera and slowly bring
The landscape into focus. My heart stutters
But my hand is firm, and as I click the shutter
I feel the cold blood thawing in my veins.

*

I see you standing there, not quite full length.
Successive sheets of ice preserve and bear
You up, first as a girl with wavy hair,
And then a prisoner, a skeleton
Just gathering new flesh. The layers go on
So fast that I am troubled by your strength.

But fainter now, you're sitting in a chair
And wasting away under a fall of snow.
Once more under the skin the faint bones show
Their X-rays. The fragility of ice
Is starting to break up and once or twice
The water spreads across you like fine hair,

Fine hair confusing everything, now dark,
Now light, whichever way the double vision
Catches it. I'm angling for position,
Betraying you with your own camera.
The winter offers vague ephemera
And leaves behind no trace or watermark.

There's nothing to betray. I am exposed
And doubled. I have grown two-faced, split skins,
Become a multiple. Something begins
To bother me – I think it's my own voice.
The situation offers me no choice –
The shutter's open. Now the shutter's closed.

Voluptuousness

I think of a child dancing along a faint chalk line;
the sound of his feet, the flop of his hair, and his breath
a short skipping rhyme of tumbling aspirates.

The small knotted belly, the slightly sweating thigh,
the damp neck and palm, and nearby on a bench
a mother or elder sister rich in voluptuousness.

My sister is an enclosed garden. In the garden
the soft wickerwork of worm casts, black earth nipped
into buds, scored into clefts and crevices.

On windy ways a dancing underground.
Inside the bones unsettling swathes of thought,
the mind exposed to crisp surgical fingers

that pinch it into song, the local floods
of swollen veins whose banks cannot contain
their discontent. I think of my two children

swept along those waves, arriving where they are
at pianos and computers, before their mirrors,
their eyes illegible, a foreign writing.

I was once a child too, leaning over the edge of the pram,
examining my brother like a specimen, with my mother
behind the lens, her face hidden, rich in voluptuousness.

The Swimmers

Inside the church the floor is like black ice:
The past moves underneath it as it glimmers
In the light of the long windows, and you read
In brass the images of the dead swimmers.

Shoal on shoal, the fluidity of bodies
Supports the weight of the whole edifice.
The names, resemblances and epithets
Run by beneath your feet, under the ice.

Nowhere more than in churches are you aware
Of treading water. Surely you must sink
Under the weight of your own body: the building
Itself becomes nebulous and starts to shrink,

But the swimming goes on undisturbed. The dead
Press water and each other down the centuries
Of darkness: dear small girls, their sisters, mothers,
Husbands, families, their towns, whole countries

Float in the river which runs steadily
Dissolving everything. No wonder
The churches smell of damp and sadness.
The present drips from walls, the rest go under.

*

Like Venables Hinde, infant of the parish,
Along with John, Martha and Bess, of whom
None lived beyond thirty, though each lived longer
Than seven infant Hindes in the same tomb.

History is prodigal with numbers
And Venables Hinde was simply singular:
I think of him now drifting in his coffin,
Properly snuffed, tucked and rectangular,

With solemn messages about him; warnings,
Talismans, to *Remember Eternity,*
Or else to *Redeem Time,* or a plain *Here Lieth.*
For truisms we have immense capacity

And Venables had not yet grown out of them,
A small round passive cliché, hardly elliptical,
His utterances flat and loud, mere noise
Between one or other mortal receptacle.

Poor swimmers, hardly strength enough to move
And yet constrained to buttress a whole chapel.
Tread lightly here, respect the concentration
Of these verbose and delicate people.

*

Who's lost, who's found? I've looked here for you sometimes
And tried to feel such correspondences
As time redeems, remembering... I've strained
To hear you speak coherent sentences,

Cloud-cuckoo tongues, High Dutch or a pure Greek,
A tongue as washed out and as disinfected
As the water; full of hesitations
And precise declensions, but quite unaffected.

How foreign they all sound. How far downstream
From the familiar parish. Their formal prose
Has stiffened into marble but the tongues
Wag on, like plants, in a tide that comes and goes...

Drowned hands and skin; the water drifting off
Becoming water. Their bodies are unknown
As are the names you lived by. Who'll lay claim
To this faint draft of skin, this line of bone?

Whose element is water? A vacuous bright room
Waits upstairs. You approach it quietly –
Like rising through the sea and hearing nothing –
No names, no objects, no singing, nothing but sea.

*

Some forty years ago a girl was drowning
In the icy Danube, one of a great number
Shot that day in the last week of the Terror.
Time and again she seemed to have gone under,

But rose once more, raising a stiff arm.
Between the floes she drifted perilously,
A patch of flesh. Some die hard like cats,
And a cat was what she was most obviously.

But cats as swimmers? Yes, a miracle,
Her jaw shot half away, how she pressed forward.
The Danube was as dullish red as she:
That single arm conveyed the creature shoreward.

Those who remained below grew slippery
And featureless. Unfortunate the disparity
Between high-fliers and the deeply drowned.
She had something of an angel's clarity.

I hear that splashing as they throw her in,
The ripples spreading grey and red and white
From the small body, echoing in the stone.
The hymns begin. The cats sing in the night.

The Swimming Pool in the House

There's a swimming pool in the house – yes, I can smell it,
And it isn't a Roman bath or British one –
It is the water coming up to meet you,
The chlorine lapping in the August sun:
And look, an arm is waving! There's the roof
Returning all the light it does not need
To make the shadows greener, and the splash
Of bodies falling into waves that bleed
A green and hesitant curl.
                                        I was young
With the men that swam here once, and the stone
On which they stretched rose hot and angled square,
A surface we could run on though alone,
Each separate in his own patch of brown –
The skin of age unpeeling where they drown.

Dwellings

The first was a flat with a courtyard
Several rungs below the piano-room
(Dust stuck in the window there)
Where rust and chalk climbed in a spiral
Of grotesques both round and porcupine.
Children ran together in that courtyard
Their voices stripping paintwork in low rooms.

The second was a cottage, utterly filthy,
With the saving grace of black morello cherries,
Our dead lights. The hill was stained with them.
They ran or rolled down slopes between the trees
And stopped, lost between house and house,
Loaves a mile long under their stiff arms.

The next was a civilised room. Books hugged
In cabinets, a file for papers, and a wireless
Turning its ear to the loud town. A decent
Darkness spread over the corners. Their heads
Were neat and tapered, hair brushed flat,
Guardian spirits of the wall.
But dust stuck in the window there
Whenever bells rang which was not often.

Now everything is quiet. The bus snorts
Along flat roads between a set of fields;
Chalked walls indicate a choir of trees
In a park perhaps, stacked in neatest rows.
Leaving both behind, small rooms present
Their shrinking surfaces; enamelled baths,
The sliding mirrors of a cabinet,
And a body hanging with showered age,
The skin glistening.

Short Wave

1

Somewhere in there, in a gap between a taxi
and some indecipherable station
there is a frequency that's unfrequented
like an island, an administration
of ethereal incompetence, the voice of Caliban
deserted but with remnants of quaint speech,
an accent or two that could be out of Shakespeare.

You tune in but the voice is out of reach
and seems merely to flirt with meaning; dry trees
rattling on an unprotected hillside,
hollow tubes wind whistles through. It speaks
at length through a protracted landslide.

Whoever lives here, the transmitting tower
is out of date, there is no programme schedule
to list what may be listened to, what hour
the one clear and intelligible accent
will burst like a soprano voice along
the curving sea between the taxi, France
and Germany, all Europe in her song.

2

This landscape is eternal night – not hell
or purgatory, just a weave of streets
settling like a cobweb late at night
in greys and greens, advances and retreats.

Only drunkards reel home, slam the door
and wander over to the wireless
to turn the dial in hope of finding music,
celestial and perfect more or less.

3

These reasonable voices going on
and on, unconscionably long
at all hours of the day and night
mean nothing in most places, not to me.
I speak no Dutch or Spanish, tell the truth
I only know my native tongue and French
and that barely sufficient to get by with.

My lips are sour with lager and my head
has no room for a second studio.
Anyway, what do they mean, these voices?
What are they saying? Well, it can be guessed.
Which is why I sit here listening
and turning dials, eavesdropping
on that Balkan baritone
who tells me what the world believes of me.

4

The planets click like doors or whistle wide.
Their secret messages are understood
by fascinated children in their beds
who're used to lack of sleep and solitude.
Downstairs the broken speech of moving objects
where unrestricted chaos rules the air
and mother is no different from a chair.

We leave the children sleeping and ourselves
lie reading and half listening until
the close-down, when we kiss and frontiers blur
in line with international good will.
There are so many stations on the line,
and other music wells up in the drought
in waves that cancel one another out.

Busby Berkeley in the Soviet Union

1

It's the Ministry of Culture Symphony Orchestra,
a sly and dangerous band of men
living in Stalin's greatcoat, with Dmitri
Shostakovich jammed into one pocket, Beria
into another. Distant echoes of glittery
ballrooms and a harvest moon

where a silent snake of Conga dancers grinds out figures
of eight to routines impeccably
transferred from Berkeley in true Soviet spirit –
sinister choruslines consisting of beggars
and blondes in collusion, employed by the KGB.
Together yet separate

in each square of space, they spin to light froth, coagulate
to stiff geometries, symbolic
of the will of the party and people. With set
expressions of joy they're working to liquidate
whatever is louche, undisciplined or chaotic.
Forests of arms and legs float

or crystalline marble. They're playing a waltz in the pit,
terpsichorean labourers, miners
of melody, glossy anonymous ranks
of Stakhanovites, brigades of polish and spit.
Light, anaesthetic, sexy, a row of binliners
in satin rises and sinks.

The girls flash thighs and high pale knickers, ingratiating
and threatening at once. We dance on
brittle but enchanted legs. The nightmare years
are back, more seductive than ever, aching,
lyrical. Outside, undesirables have begun
to gather. The walls have ears.

2

This music is in your blood, slithering through your arteries.
It's no longer 1934
but whatever you want. Call it today if
it pleases you. You're watching TV, some series
about hospitals or cops, an investigator
on the scent or a plaintiff

in a court case or a documentary about fish,
it doesn't matter what kind of tripe
you fancy, you get it all, good quality.
So you think you are safe, but under the rubbish
it raises its head. Sweet music. Suddenly you wipe
your face. Electricity

courses through you, or is it nostalgia? Insidious
and creepy, you hear it mount the stair
like desire. It makes you feel horny, childlike,
delighted. It's like going out to the pictures
on a rainy night when water catches in your hair
and the yellow streetlights strike

along the puddles. You shut your eyes and see regiments
of soldiers or dancers shuffling by
and know they're beckoning for you to join them.
The glamour's irresistible, the sounds and scents
of the crowd, you're taking your part in a tragedy
or marching to an anthem

drunk yet disciplined, Dionysiac, in the triumph
of your will or somebody else's,
the people's, the state's, the zeitgeist's, direct
and certain, carried along in the mighty oomph
of the band as it marches past familiar houses,
impeccable, bright, correct.

The Manchurian Candidate

Imagine your own thoughts are not your own,
that you're a puppet waiting for a sign,
some secret signal, which will set you off
down preordained paths along a narrow line
unrecognisable to you, a way unknown
except within your nerves. This is the stuff
of nightmares, and your Laurence Harvey face
stares strenuously back, half out of place.

Imagine a small town in the Midwest:
one day you are confronted by a mass
of slimy matter, a blob that comes and eats
folk's innards out and monstrously can pass
through windows, walls and doors. Perhaps it's best
not to think of this. And soon the thing retreats
into its hidden spacecraft, disappears
for months at a time, or even a few years.

Imagine a place, a clean white house, some chairs
set out on porches. This place belongs to you.
It's like a mind, fresh-washed, hung out to dry.
It smells of comfort, offers a fine view
of lawns and streets the whole neighbourhood shares.
Somewhere a neighbour's child begins to cry,
a radio blares, or you hear a woman shout,
then rain comes down to wash the memory out.

Burns Night by the Danube

(in memoriam 1956)

1

A time for slogans: know them well.
Would any of them ring a bell?
You'd recognise them by the smell,
Proust's madeleines.
They tease your tongue and cast their spell,
Invade your teens.

Unreal applause, the names on tick,
A twitching body politic,
The headaches and the waiting, sick
With apprehension:
Before you rise you feel a crick.
Pre-menstrual tension?

You read your article and smile.
Should you have frowned? It's all on file,
Your *Brief Lives* brevities beguile
Astute inspectors
Of bric-à-brac, who scan for style
With lie detectors.

If they prick, do you not bleed?
Fertility is more than seed,
A broken egg is what you need
For omelette:
Your own two may well interbreed,
Intact as yet.

Then rhythmic clapping. It's the clap.
A name in a gazette or map
Is quite sufficient to unwrap
Your furled-up flag.
Does any bull perceive the trap
In a red rag?

Who can't afford to lose their grip
Develop a stiff upper lip.
A fellow student quotes a clip,
Something or other
Concerning you. Who let it slip
About your mother?

It's Mother Nature, Mother Church
And Mother Naked. Bring the birch.
The shameless hussies who besmirch
The holy altar,
Must first be rooted out. You search
And dare not falter.

Don't count the hours. The hours don't count.
Don't count your wages. The amount
Is relative. What's paramount
Is eye and ear:
The mouth or pen the only fount
And source of fear.

2

October: funeral and feast.
The corn is in, the plot is leased,
Let earth rejoice with man and beast,
In conversation:
The food is good and the deceased
Is a sensation.

A few days in ten thousand find
Our Nevsky Prospekts packed and lined
By dazed and vaguely happy, blind
Tiresian toilers:
Tomorrow they'll be cribbed, confined,
Back at the boilers.

What's never high cannot be brought
Down with a bump, is simply caught
Short in public places. Fraught,
And prone to panic,
Its one response is highly wrought,
Morose and manic,

104

A comedy, and therefore tense
As taxes or as common sense:
Relief, as always, is immense
At every prat-fall.
The villain has his impotence,
His feline cat-call.

But everyone gets walk-on parts
In history. The action starts.
The scenes are shot. Bring on the carts,
Remove the dying.
Ill fortune flings her fatal darts,
The fur is flying.

If one could only keep all these
Safely between parentheses,
Initials carved in civic trees
To spite mere nature:
Proclaiming in telegraphese
To the vast future:

Specifics and particulars
Are everything The burned-out cars
Reveal their names. The city's scars
Are told and entered
In the records. Death appears
To have repented.

The children lying in the street
You will remember, and the feet
Protruding from beneath the sheet,
A shoe or dress.
Your own tall room, the dining suite.
The drunkenness.

The Button Maker's Tale

Once I had a shop where I made buttons,
but buttons sank like lead, without a trace.
I lost my money and I lost my buttons,
but I was young and didn't give a fig.

The next time I put money into figs,
but figs were almost unobtainable.
I lost my money and I lost my figs.
The whole affair was most embarrassing.

After that I couldn't do much better
than put my money into foreign postcards.
(Saucy postcards! Who'll buy saucy postcards?)
The moral climate changed within a year.

I can't help it. I have this sort of hunger
for risk and failure. So I took up hunger,
which wasn't then a scarce commodity –
people bought it and paid me with their curses.

So last I put my money into damns.
The time was ripe and all the tills were ringing,
my little chicks were coming home to roost.
But my lot was with damns and not with chickens.

I was waiting for the Revolution,
but when it came it caught us unprepared.
We lost our money (some of us lost lives)
and ceased to trade at all, except in jokes,

of which this story is a specimen.
You'll not deny it has a certain length
generous for the times, and, much like buttons,
serves to hold these tattered clothes together.

The Courtyards

1

As if a mind subsumed its intellect,
an ear tuned in to noise within the skull,
a mouth spoke words of greeting to a dull
audience of teeth, or an eye observed
the rigging of its fibres and the curved
elastic walls where images collect;

as if a street had turned its stately back
on public matters, and had found a way
of contemplating its own poverty,
had rattled up its years of emptiness
and counted them out on an abacus
of winding stairs, or on a curtain track;

the small lift shuts and forces itself up
a narrow throated shaft with groans of chains
and pulleys, and the whole building complains;
but as you rise through slices of pale light
the brown intensifies to cream, and white,
a trancelike ring of silence at the top.

2

Think of a glove turned neatly inside out;
think of your hand running along a rail
as children run down galleries grown stale
with refuse; think of hands reversed; of keys
and locks; think of these blocks as hollow trees
still echoing to something inchoate;

think of fear, precise as a clean hand
searching in dark corners, with the skill
that years of practice manage to instil;
think of locks where keys will never turn;
of rooms where it takes experts to discern
a movement that the eye can't understand:

The inchoate is what gets lost. You hear
a crazy woman singing, ...*Tannenbaum,
O tannenbaum*... but then her words become
confused with curses, shouts of God and Fate,
and this is not exactly inchoate
but in such imprecision there is fear.

3

Outside, a rusticated, vermiform
ebullience; outside, a cluttering
of pediments, pilasters, pargeting,
embroidery; outside, the balconies
expand in their baroque epiphanies,
their splendid Biedermeyer uniforms;

outside, the casement windows under rolls
of stonework, rough or smooth or both; façades
with manners courtly as old playing cards;
outside, the straining figures stiffly bent
to hold up yet another pediment
disfigured by a web of bulletholes;

outside, the falling masonry, the hard
emphatic counter-patterns of collapse,
the shattered panes and almost hingeless flaps
that bang like toy guns to disturb the dust.
Inside, the ironwork, the lines of rust;
inside, the piles of rubble in the yard.

4

Inside, the caretaker; his wife; his cat;
a cage for small bikes; rows of potted plants
reaching for light; stuff that no one wants
left in the stairwell; little dingy signs
for manicurists, tailors; heavy lines
of washing stretched out tight from flat to flat;

inside, a sort of life. At one o'clock
the ringing feet of children up the stair,
the scrape of chalk where someone scrawls a bare
diagrammatic girl with breasts like bells
and leaves a message in rough capitals;
inside, the noisy opening of locks.

Inside, I think of someone else, a blind
and aged woman treading the fourth floor
as if it were a jetty from a shore
suspended in a band of warming light.
She feels her way to the door opposite.
The hollow building trembles in her hand.

5

Think of an empty room with broken chairs,
a woman praying, someone looking out
and listening for someone else's shout
of vigilance; then think of a white face
covered with fine powder, bright as glass,
intently looking up the blinding stairs.

There's someone moving on a balcony;
there's someone running down a corridor;
there's someone falling, falling through a door,
and someone firmly tugging at the blinds.
Now think of a small child whom no one minds
intent on his own piece of anarchy:

Think of a bottle lobbing through the air
describing a tight arc – one curious puff –
then someone running, but not fast enough.
There's always someone to consider, one
you have not thought of, one who lies alone,
or hangs, debagged, in one more public square.

6

As if the light had quietly withdrawn
into a state of grace; as if the sun
had moved out to the country, or had gone
abroad; as if the shadows had grown old
and grey, or found their recesses too cold
and spread themselves across a civic lawn.

Then what is left? I see the woman grip
the handrail as she feels her way along.
She clutches fervently a ball of string,
an old steel key. She turns the corner, calls
to someone downstairs; and the steel key falls,
suspended like an odd metallic drip.

As if the past could ever lose its teeth:
As if the eye could swallow everything
and leave the world in darkness, blundering
about the courtyards! As if all the words
not spoken here could congregate like birds
and block out the faint noises from beneath!

7

Uncertainly she calls out from the top
of the thin stairs. The key won't fit the lock.
The key won't turn. The key is firmly stuck
inside the door. Then how to get up there
but run up every storey by the stair,
and hope she'll still be there when the stairs stop,

and hope she'll still be there when the stairs stop.

Day of the Dead, Budapest

Down the main arterials, on ring roads, in alleyways,
The dead stand perpendicular with heads ablaze.
And some of them blow out, while others burn right down
And leave small patches of darkness like footsteps about town.

The House Stripped Bare by Her Bachelors, Even

The outer layers are gone. The houses shiver
in brick underwear. They feel the shame of it.
Their iron bones embarrass them. The river
has worn them down and left them bare,
all edges and splinter, wispy as maidenhair.

They are softer than they think. Fingers of lead
have probed their sides, shells dug them in the ribs.
Friable earth, they crumble into gutters,
shower with white dust the blind head
of the man in the doorway, wave broken shutters
at each other like so many soiled bibs.

The bachelors who stripped them bare are blowing
about the street with sweetpapers and other ephemera,
seedy old raincoats lost in a dust haze,
who hesitate, vaguely aware of where they are going
humming an air from a pre-war opera,
if only they could think of the name of it.

The Idea of Order at the József Attila Estate

The lawns are in order, someone is keeping them neat.
No one has yet tipped rubbish down from the tenth floor.
People are walking their dogs or waiting for buses
As if they had taken to heart the architect's fiction of order,
And saw their own lives in exploded and bird's eye views.

It all has an explanation. The woman once sentenced to death,
The silver beard of the courier-spy, the pentathlete,
The shrunken delicacy of the woman with the zimmer frame:
These lives fit together as if in a programme, a drawing
In a department, one all-embracing stroke of genius.

The lifts rise like zips. They do up the block which maintains
The sealed and communal weather of its residents.
It is peaceful and calm in their versions of being,
A dream of files and cabinets at uniform temperature
Where death entails merely a comfortless distancing,

Something diffuse, clouds seen from the roof garden,
Thousands of breathing cells misting up windows,
Waste materials flushed down arterial pipeways,
The voices of children scrambling upstairs,
And the distant suburban railway coming and going.

Border Crossing

You leave one body, enter another, thinner than
The one you wore. Having nothing to declare
The customs do not bother you. You pass
To other gravities, no longer man or woman,
But neuter as the clothes you wear
As thin and transparent as glass.

In the glass you see anatomies,
Bacteria and germs in broken places.
You see the future in slivers and shards,
Faint, farcical lobotomies.
I try to discover my disease in traces
Of tea leaves, life-lines, livers, tarot cards.

Impossible to read the auguries:

The future waits on fiercer surgeries.

Anthropomorphosis

Foreigners, said the lady. Off the bus
Fell two dark men in heavy duty jackets.
The conductor swore; a pair of dogs
Leapt after a ball in gusts of fretful barking.
The men stood at the kerb watching the bus
Disappear over the crest of the hill, then turned
Sharply and walked off in the opposite direction
Pausing only for one to let fly with a gob
Of spit toward the curving wall behind them.

It was as if I'd seen it all before –
That long sail of spit arching over.
By my will I held it there, suspended
Between brick and mouth. Slowly some
Indefinite memory broke, spilling its garbage:
A harbour town smelling of dead fish,
The uncertainty of leaving mingled with
Excitement at arrival. Years of water
Concentrated to a blob of spit
On its trajectory, and the afternoon
Rearranged itself around his act.

And though I could not say what place it was
Or how long ago, I too hung there
Encapsulated in that quick pearled light,
Spewed by his volition, about to crack,
The taste of sea already penetrating my mouth.

Foresters

Cameron, and his morbid fascination
With gremlins, water-spirits and outlanders
Had them pinned and mounted, a sour nation
Of fearful superstitious peasants
Who drifted into town out of the forests
In search of fresh sea-air and giant crow's-nests,
Talked of vampires and the lycanthrope
And used these comic horrors to scare the pants
Off naughty children and give hope
To balding office wolves for whom
A white neck spelt invariable doom.

But Cameron forgot to give this nation
Credit for their gift of adaptation.
Who faced the baleful gods now faced the sea
And made a certain noise even in the city
And gained success as gatherers of samphire
By infusing native charm with touches of the vampire.

Assassins

My people, by whom I mean those curious sets
Of non-relations in provincial towns,
Sit ripening brightly in the *Weltanschauung*
Of other poets. Here is one who follows
A second-hand pair of shoes into the Courts
Of Social History. Another ransacks
His late unlettered father's bedside drawer
And finds dead ukuleles littered there.
What heraldic yet surreal landscapes!
To lie in the bed of your ancestors
And feel the fit. To hear the neighbourhood
Stirring in its ancient sleep and rhyme
The dead into their regiments of pain.
The poverty of old shoes runs away
With its own eloquence. And yet they write good books.

But I think of an England where the ghosts
Are restless solitaries or assassins.
They cannot speak but run about in sunlight
Demanding restoration of the birch
And death as public as the crime is private.
They have lost time. The Russians on Burns night
Celebrate their history of combustions.
Their people lie in complete unity
In graves as large as Europe and as lonely.

A Picture of My Parents with Their First Television

I see them before the television, the proud owners
of a wooden case in which the four-o-five
presents its milky versions of success
with the last official faces of a time
that was always more dead than alive,
when Hanratty cleaned the windows and a crime
was solved by men with briefcases and bowlers,
when gentlemen made jokes in evening dress.

They fought their way to this, to Lady Barnett
to Bernard Braden and John Freeman, Kathie Kay
and Alan Breeze, to all those names of power
that solved nothing but could somehow fill
the hours before they slipped away
to private lives which grew more private still,
past old reliable faces by which they set
their clocks precisely to the latest hour.

Some blurred depth in their eyes won't come to rest:
perhaps they're trapped in what they bought,
in all their trappings, in the slim white frame
of the square photograph they sent back home
to show the television. Now they're caught
and solemn. Slowly they become
the stillness by which they are both possessed.
They're listening intently for a name

which once had power, on lips that formed the sound
in darkened flats, in beds in which they slept
and touched each other. Some act of violence
has pitched them here before the screen.
The actors know their speeches, are adept
at pulling faces, know when to go. They've been
elsewhere and are there still, on neutral ground,
of which this patch of grey is evidence.

English Words

My first three English words were AND, BUT, SO:
they were exotic in my wooden ear,
like Froebel blocks. Imagination made
houses of them, just big enough to hang
a life on. Genii from a gazetteer
of deformations or a *sprechgesang*:
somehow it was possible to know
the otherness of people and not be afraid.

Once here, the words arranged their quaint occasions,
Minding their Manners, Waiting in the Queues
at Stops and Hatches. I got to know their walls,
their wallpaper and decorative styles,
their long louche socks, their sensible scuffed shoes.
Peculiar though: their enigmatic smiles
and sideways looks troubled my conversation
swimming in clouds above the steam of kettles.

You say a word until it loses meaning
and taste the foreignness of languages,
your own included. Sheer inanity
of idiom: the lovely words are dead,
their magic gone, evaporated pages.
But this too is a kind of spell: unread,
the vocables coagulate and sting,
glow with their own electricity.

I cannot trust words now. One cultivates
the sensuous objects in a locked museum:
their sounds are dangerous and must be heard
voluptuously, but behind thick glass.
Their emptiness appals one. One is dumb
with surprise at their inertia, their crass
hostility. They are beautiful opiates,
as brilliant as poppies, as absurd.

Necromancy

It was the daughter-in-law not the son
Who felt the mother kissing her one night.
She had been dead three years. Curiously
He slept. He never could remember dreams.
His hand moved in a slime of known events
Intangible as dreams. A live thing hovered
In the room with the casual ease of air,
Obeying her, though not his, necromancy:
Blood coloured curtains, blankets rucked like tombs,
The bed was soft, the earth fell outwards gently,
Sheets wound as sheets will, folds pushed with manners
Into folds of body, sinking. They were all waves,
An affection without hope like desire.

Half Light

She is standing in a darkness that is luminous,
I say, but my cat flicks her green eyes upward
as if to reply, That is a lie, darkness cannot
be luminous unless I choose to make it so,
and she who is standing there inhabits darkness.
That argument is appropriate: I no longer know
who that woman might be. A dark croon of traffic
sings in my ears; plaster and brick
are four-square, both physical and mental space.
Yet someone is standing, waiting quietly
making that darkness luminous. I riffle
through my acquaintance, dead or living. A mother
dead too early burned brightly enough it is true
but would scarcely deign to blow to such thin flame
that darkness itself was the more noticeable –
Whose fingers if not hers then scratch away
behind the lids, causing the sensation of light?

As I Was Going Up the Stair

As I was going up the stair
I met a woman made of air
who seemed a creature half asleep
struggling dreamlike up the steep
demanding incline which would lead
eventually to her bed.
   It seemed to her a dreadful cliff
which she must climb however stiff
and breathless she became, as if
it only mattered to attain
the landing and be free of pain.
   But she was proud to be alone
and pleased to be dependent on
nothing but a wooden rail
between two floors, and this was all
that seemed to her desirable.
It was indeed a kind of game
terminal and dangerous.

Though rooms vary from house to house
most staircases are much the same;
I passed her almost at a run
and when I turned round she was gone.

Recording

A distant night train and a dog. Then crickets.
And fingers turning the leaves of a book.
Insects hover at the window. The hedges lean back.
Their curving arms are paths of rockets.

The final sensations are necessarily fragmentary,
like voices on a tape recorder repeating...
and there's the horror. Somebody goes on quoting
fragments, unattributable, without memory.

THE FLIES

On a Winding Staircase

I climb these stairs which might be by Vermeer.
Light drools like spittle from the rails. They wind
towards a window, and even from down here
I make out the faint iron bands that bind
the house together in one act of will.

The writing on the wall says *Carpe Dym*
attached to the name of a national hero, or
it could well be the local football team.
Upstairs are voices I have heard before
that hook and draw you up as on a line,

to something cramped, imprisoned and defined
by yards and corridors. I run my hand
along the wall and feel it sweat and grind
its teeth. A brilliant light is in command,
a fist of light within an iron frame.

One purpose, one cohesion. People spill
from monumental gateways, accidents
of sun and shadow, leaving at their peril
the fortress of controllable events,
venturing out and over the world's rim.

I wait to see a family descend
down thirty years, each of them framed alone
before the window as they comprehend
the force that welds them with the light in one
unbreakable and static composition.

They owe a debt to history, that calm
and droning music which slows to a dead march.
Look at these maps, as wrinkled as a palm,
repoussoir instruments, an antique arch,
a girl with a trumpet, bent on playing *Fame*.

The Coolest Room in the City

This is the coolest room in the city,
three windows see to that, and leaves
like dark stains
lend a kind opacity
through which the whole room breathes,
and later when it rains

the windows answer anxiously,
knock for knock, and let the damp
cloud up the panes;
a cataract through which we see
reflections of a lamp
lit only when it rains.

Rooms are at their friendliest
when keeping something out. To sleep
is best. Bright chains
of water dangling at the breast
preserve their calm and keep
silence when it rains.

Rain

Rain all night. Those sitting in the roof
can hear it talking but they cannot tell
the nature of its message.
It broods and blows, gathers, grows smooth
and seamless. In the stairwell
and the basement passage

it spreads as damp, the closing smell of sweat.
A fly is buzzing round and round. You wouldn't think
a creature small as that
could emit so thick a blare. It deals in threat
and sings of filth. You seem to hear the stink
of old outhouses and dried shit.

Those who speak are moving in the houses,
closing doors, wiping their faces. One picks up
a paper, another puts one down.
Familiar looks, good nights. A car cruises
by outside. Lost and out of step,
history leaves the empty town.

The rain is a mad typist clattering out
endless streams of letters without a break,
littered with quaint symbols
You can't pronounce the words, nor can you shout
for lack of vowels. The language starts to ache
and slowly crumbles.

If rain talks it talks nonsense. We lie beside
each other on the bed and think of all
who lie there listening.
Bodies and bodies and the rain outside.
The small intimate whispers of the wall.
The loud fly's translucent wing.

Drawing the Curtain

'Observe the convolutions of this frieze.'
The voice comes to me like a tourist guide
explaining the explicable.
To slide your hand behind the stucco, seize
the mortar and move gently round inside
makes sensuous and tangible.

Curved galleries like zips, a moral fall
of stairs and liftshafts, and the flickering
inconsequentiality
of every human movement – material
and light – make an expanding, shapeless ring
of meaning and capacity.

An accident defines what breaks the heart –
the history of architecture, not of form
but aberration, lapse of taste,
the way an elevation tears apart
its brick integument before the storm
that lays the human pattern waste.

It is quite possible to love a face
the moment it appears and then is lost
in the darkness within windows, shut
within the belly of the commonplace,
that achieves the equivocation of a ghost
or a telephone with wires cut.

It turns to radios barely heard, until
the loud convergence of external moments
threatening familiar sound,
when history packs her bags and pays the bill
long owing, and the intimate events,
the lives of chairs and beds, are drowned.

Compulsive patterns of crude ironwork
in the glass panel of a door, the dangerous
geometry of aerials
on roofs the colour of air, and every quirk,
irregularity, each hint of madness,
are her discarded materials.

The miracles of value, allegiance, loss
are hardly different from a moving curtain.
A hand appears and a shape holds
a single space before they're drawn across,
and in that movement everything uncertain
hurts and gathers in the folds.

A Domestic Faust

Now come into the room. Turn on the light.
It's almost evening. Make yourself a drink.
The hiss of gas and the faint lisp
of match on sandpaper, the sudden bright
crown of quotidian fire, and then the sink
with answering crown and cusp;

the thrust of water like a rod of glass
that stuns enamel with its arrogance;
the breaking up and filling out,
the borborygmus of containers; mass,
acceleration, smell and permanence,
the ordinariness without

that turns to ordinariness within
in homely physics, domesticity.
Even of danger. When you strike
your head on a cupboard door or cut your skin
on paper you excite a kind of pity,
person and place being too alike.

You could be anywhere. Indeed you are
and always have been. It is where you go,
a mini-Mephistopheles,
a footling Faustus with familiar.
What ho, apprentice! What is there to know?
You are the master with the keys

to your own secret universe: a drawer,
a hidden box, addresses, numbers, names
and letters. All the magic charms
that gain you entrance to the inner core
of nothing/everything, the language games,
the smell of your underarms.

And far out there, responsibility
to every piece of unforgiving matter.
You run your hands across the bed
and look out from your window on the city,
draw the curtain, face the daily clutter
of the body beneath your head,

which I can't see from where I sit and gaze.
I know you are there, somewhere above
the traffic, neither near nor far
but in the middle distance which displays
a darkened rectangle that I must love
for itself and not for what we are.

A Woman with a Rug

Three loud cracks. A woman with a rug
is beating it against the rails. A rich green
flares and droops from her hands, then snap!
it's gone. It is as if she'd pulled the plug
on the street: everything is quiet again,
back within its trap.

In the nearby theatre Tuzenbach's on fire
with one of his neurotic rhapsodies.
Irina draws away from him.
He's ugly and half German. They quickly tire
of his lolloping anxiety. They tease
him because he is vague and dim

even in a passion. He seems to miss
the tragic dimension which is rightly theirs,
their words and images,
the poems embedded in their memories.
He drifts and stumbles among chairs
down unlit passages

of dialogue. Meanwhile the woman tucks
the rug under her arm and looks across
in one of those lost moments
that can't be measured by the usual clocks,
so immobile and permanent, its loss
will never be noted in documents.

Neither will this. This moment and the next
have splintered into far too many sharp
small fragments. Unreclaimable
the bright green rug, the Baron's buried text.
Vermeer waits while time begins to warp
around his carpet-covered table

between the curtain and the string of pearls
held to the light but never quite in focus.
Irina, Masha, Olga freeze
against wild grass which has no time for girls.
The world of things remains as various
and indifferent as the leaves

in the garden which itself is lost, and where
the band is gaily signalling the fracture
of a life. A single crack is heard.
The human voice surrenders to the air:
the rug flares in the trap, its architecture
hangs clear and then is quickly blurred.

The Flies

Forgive this garrulousness. As I write
a fat black fly crawls up the windowpane.
He feels the winter's over. Spring
anticipates itself and sets alight
worn patches of grass. The promise of warm rain
is like veins on a fly's wing.

And now the fly drops past the radiator.
The time is wrong for him. He scrambles up
fizzing furiously, leans
against the glass, revving up his motor,
then into gear and upwards. He can't stop
and think. His legs are small machines

that run until run down. I let him out.
The dot grows quickly smaller, disappears
in detail, in the dappled air.
Two distant birds swoop down and wheel about,
no bigger than flies. If I strain my ears
I hear their automatic whirr.

Look far enough, the human flies emerge...
I can't maintain this game of telescopes,
having never been a god
or sportsman though the hunting urge
lives in me too. I know the black fly gropes
towards his notion of the good,

his personal heap, however much it stinks;
that being here is an aesthetic choice
for those who have it, and for now
we are among this few. What the wall thinks
is my concern. We give the wall a voice.
The cut worm forgives the plough

and to the fly the plough is the cold wind
brewing beyond the Buda hills, the frost
making a belated entrance.
It's not the business of weather to be kind
nor of the market visitor to count the cost
of gypsies and of peasants.

Eternal polished faces a few streets off,
clutching embroidery or dogs for sale,
their arguments and raucous cries
exhorting us to buy the useless stuff
of lives which from here quickly lose their scale,
grow small and disappear like flies.

A Sea Change

Far down below in next door's yard a heap
of part-dismembered cookers. On the sixth floor
shelves of plants like trailing wires
and old toupees. They've entered the big sleep,
said long goodbyes. But that's not all, there's more,
the winter merely stores desires

under the bed, in envelopes or tins.
It is a time of scuttling, wrapping close,
watching the waves of pigeons beat
against cold air. Even now something begins,
if ever so quietly, something so various
it is impossible to repeat,

that happens only once each time, perhaps
once any lifetime, a sea change so immense
we cannot see it happen but
no one can stop thinking about it. The maps
are restless, all the boundaries are tense;
they have this feeling in the gut.

On the playground pingpong table someone scrawls
the words *New Fascists* with terrible irony.
The fearful and the ugly stalk
the spring as always. The fog's white terror calls
at dawn, remains with us. Its tyranny
lends dark edges to our talk,

but that won't stop us talking, listening.
The university bells begin to toll,
the central heating gurgles and ticks,
the starling chatters on and telephones ring
in nearby rooms. The world is audible
at last above its politics

and talks to itself. Behind the frosted glass
someone takes a shower. These things are done
precisely as before but feel
a little different now. The yellow grass
is its own particular shade. The railings run
more purposefully and reveal

precise configurations in the gaps.
It matters that you give things the right name
and measure their extent, their power.
It happens rarely. Now's the time perhaps
for understanding what remains the same.
The water thunders in the shower.

In a Strong Light

Behind the shower-curtain thunder sharpens
into light. The douche destroys
the human figure and does its best
to murder space. Everything that happens
is the echo of something else, which merely deploys
your shoulder and your breast.

The white striations shimmer without contour
exhaled in the relieved sigh
of water. You dissolve in pools.
The sun breaks on bare twigs in a winter
truce between opposing powers of grey.
Even as the body cools

the room still breathes its freshness and the scent
of soap continues to haunt the walls. Alone
the body loses resolution,
and feels at home in its abandonment.
The lost flesh settles down against the bone
with the lightness of a cushion.

To feel complete and disparate at once
is rarely possible. Think how the sun
breaks down a house yet makes it glow
in burning fragments or deconstructs a fence
into mere rhythm. All the harmony is gone,
but something leaps where shadows throw

their careless and flat members. Your body is warm
and slopes so gently. Hands have narrowed it
to wrists and ankles, formed the bolder
curvatures of your temple and your arm,
explored your ears, lovingly parodied
your brittle collarbone and shoulder.

To snap out of the body, find it stiff
or burned or crippled, to become objective
as sun or water are, will not
completely cancel out a world. And if
it did there'd still remain the live
arguments of the planet:

the child in the pushchair; quiet empty places
where the streets are full of dogshit; hats and shoes;
grotesques met in an underpass;
the delicate careful pity of faces
in memory or mirror; the everyday news
of bridges, trees and grass.

A Game of Statues

The pond seems to be still, but everywhere
small points of tension gather and stretch.
Dead leaves float in cowls.
The slab breaks up. The foil begins to tear.
The grass is smeared with snowdrops, bluebells, vetch.
The air is a parliament of fowls.

Broad avenues and city parks are dressed
to kill. Houses put on airs and graces.
A hidden population of statues
emerges from the shadows to be pressed
between the brickwork till the terraces
are packed with ancient vices and virtues

pouting and posturing. Their breasts and biceps curve
against the sunlight which first called them out,
even the crippled ones assume
survival rights. Forsaking their reserve,
they brandish their stigmata. Blank faces shout
from pediments, burst into bloom.

An air of celebration. Time replies
with memory. She mounts a ruined staircase
through heaps of rubble. She has come
back from the camps and wagons to surprise
the world. Each broken window wears her face,
her footsteps are a muffled drum.

She knows what she has to do. No need for food,
affection is the cure: the street's hot breath
on neck and earlobe, words and sighs.
They let her go. The air in the room is good
but better still to pass through it, through death,
to this demi-paradise

of iron, stone and stucco. Across the city
thousands are marching past, and poking heads
and arms through niches, waiting there
for common symbols of eternity.
Think of them struggling in their vertical beds
against the continual nightmare

of the wall. The whole street seems to pose
and catch the light. Across the ruffled pond
birds are frozen into screams
of joy. A single, vaguely comatose
statue holds real flowers in her hand.
The flowers are dying as she dreams.

Street Entertainment

The March wind turns up suddenly and shreds
loose canvas on the awnings. Inverted flames
of cloth billow and long to escape
the world of definitions. Even people's heads
seem to be on fire, grow lion's manes,
echoing some comical shape

of terror. These are territorial wars.
You half expect them to rise and spit at each other
just as the rain is doing now,
to arch their backs and growl. Well, here are cars
hunched and growling, part of the same weather,
low clouds learning to bellow

with best or worst. You should have expected this.
You should have worn your coat or slipped the brolly
into your pocket. They are so neat,
so easy to carry. The weather has given notice
it intends to change. It thinks of human folly
as a faint tickling under its feet.

The street entertainers are out. One old beggar
blows his harmonica so faintly the sound
is blown back in his face. A boy
with a recorder stands before a figure
of Mercury, with his schoolcap on the ground
like an abandoned toy.

The ones that interest me are a pair
dressed vaguely as musketeers, in puritan hats
and rose pink gowns. They wield
long sticks. They do nothing but stare
at the growing crowd, till someone puts
a coin into the box, when a wild

mechanical movement seizes them and they
are frozen once again in attitudes
of sinister aggression.
Their faces mimic something, yet are empty.
A girl runs between them and poses. The crowd
laughs at her silly expression.

I'm merely a reporter whose truth lies
in diction clear as water. In the pool
which I imagine by my shoes
I try to see my features, read my eyes.
It ripples. My face is indistinguishable,
the water darkens like a bruise.

National Anthem

The spring begins an age of festivals:
the outbreaks and foundations, liberations,
appointed days, appointed modes
of putting on. The flags hang from the walls.
The weather bustles by. The operations
of the state. The empty roads.

The corridors too are empty though the sun
has laid its fingers underneath each door
to beckon us out. It's quiet:
something bothers the sky. Something remains undone.
April now but it could be May: Nature
that great abstraction is set

before us: small green arguments of leaves,
the proclamations of blossom on each branch,
the flowers with their furious dance.
Meaning! Meaning! they jostle, Whoever believes
in us, must give us meaning! An avalanche
of meaning! Let us have significance!

They shimmer and shake in silence before windows,
in tall black rectangles beyond which only
gods and geometricians see.
I too am sitting in one. Windows close
and open, doors swing to. There is nobility
in loneliness and vacancy,

but meaning too is rooted in a place,
is like a statue always looking past
the same old clump of trees
winter and summer, the same look on its face.
How long can faces at the windows last?
They disappear by slow degrees

each disappearance quick in its own terms.
Mother, father, child. They call out names
that no one understands but them.
They wear their universal forms,
their worn-out clothes. The sunlight frames
each figure like a theorem.

We're here, such as we are. We will be missed.
Some children gather opposite, look down
into the courtyard where
music's playing. A lone saxophonist
proffers the national anthem. The notes are blown
random, slow, into the air.

Chinese White

Do you remember that scene in Ashes and Diamonds *where*
the hero rushes forward through the clotheslines and bleeds
to death among the sheets? Or was it
in Canal *(I can't remember now.) A square*
of white turns slowly red. The redness fades
to black and white. The picture is a composite,

a form of poster. The War, the Resistance,
something about betrayal, all mixed up
in a child's mind who didn't see
the war, for whom it is a haunting presence
of sheets and blood. An image hangs and drops
in a grey passageway or alley.

His name was Zbigniew, and he wore dark glasses,
and later he jumped from a train (a true life fact)
because, well, Poles are like that,
they get drunk, morose, et cetera. The girl who kisses
the boy was blonde as always. Was it an act
of bravery him getting shot

or cowardice? We could look it up in books
but that is not the point (we pull our serious face)
but something in the falling, the how
and where of it. And so wherever one looks
the same old images return and find their place,
a square, an alleyway, a row

of ordinary houses suddenly still and hot
and people falling lying as if on a square
of film. You see the victim's head
as someone aims and shoots him, and you cut
to tanks or bodies or a sheet hung out to air,
a white square slowly turning red.

Burning Stubble at Szigliget

We stepped out on the balcony. The sky
had grown romantic and the breaking pods
and stalks were rapid volleys of light.
The air was damp, but somewhere it was dry
as fury, spitting heat. The little roads
were silent and the trees clung tight

to the black park, which had for years been theirs.
The statues held their poses even though
no one was there to see them, lost
in dark and dark grey, minding their own affairs.
The alien world lay immediately below,
and waited patient at its post.

Deep alizarin crimson, bleeding down
to ochre, orange, yellow. Spectacular
colours and a crackling rain
which wasn't rain but something overthrown.
The light was falling like the morning star:
the sons of light were dark again.

On lamp-posts, upside down, hung shrunken skins
which once were men. Tractors like tanks appeared
and crushed the street to crisp white flour.
A woman was kicking a corpse. The thin grey curtains
of smoke trembled and behind them cleared
a space for buildings and a shower

of broken stucco. A sentence broke apart,
each word a promise made in any street
and broken here. I couldn't sleep.
Beyond the park I heard the firing start
and the snap snap snap was tiny running feet
of shrews and mice, of lives held cheap.

Well, it was tidy and the cheapness ours,
our cheap hands on the pillars, our cheap eyes
seeking the heart of flames between
the foreground darkness. Now for a few hours
the fields would burn and the tall smoke would rise
as delicate as mesh to screen

the lake beyond the fields, the towns astride
the motorway, high white estates like teeth,
the factories, our balcony,
and all the others who had come outside
to stand by blazing windows ranged beneath
the rolling smoke, the thin grey sea.

Wild Garden

Vadkert. The wild garden. Sunlight. Notations
on a stave, an airless music in the ears
of bridges, masonry and trees
which spread themselves like railway stations,
heading off towards the park to hear
plain footsteps, plain itineraries.

But who are these, these wild ones in the garden,
the calves and chickens, peacocks, ducks and rams
at whom pre-conscious children wave
fistfuls of crumbs, for whom the old unburden
themselves of stale loaves? Why do the rattling trams
carry them both towards this grave

ceremonial greenness? Such incongruity
is simply another game of let's pretend
that nothing happens. It calls you back,
reminds you how you too felt gravity
tugging at your spine like an old friend
who gave you a playful smack

then set you up again. A mother waits
by an empty push-chair. Her child puts a finger through
the chicken wire. Birds peck at it
disappointed. The menagerie congregates
around us, black, white, purple, peacock blue:
brilliant and profligate.

Happiness is very simple really,
it flows out of the horn of plenty, abundant
as rain or grass but wilder, rarer
than the rainbow. Are you here with me?
Will you stand beside me for ever, as constant
as these farmyard birds and fairer

than the peacock, startled and beautiful,
with with his improbable Japanese elegance?
In the city they're counting votes
and learning how to speak. Feel gravity pull
your sleeve to closer acquaintance with all gardens.
From this distance you may make notes

on the society of worms and ants and clods
in their private infinity of lives
lived in terror of the creatures
of the garden. And beyond them lie the woods,
the lakes, the sea and the enormous waves
on which we inscribe our human features.

In Memoriam Sándor Weöres

I met him only once. So light and grey,
his handshake hardly registered. He might
have been a speck of household dust,
his absence the most palpable quality.
He settled in the chair and made a slight
noise, as if he'd caught a crust

of dry bread in his throat. He signed my book
in a childish trembling hand. He was depressed.
His cat had died. He could hardly speak
but smiled, shyly, vaguely. He had the look
of a February morning, waiting, dressed,
for some final naked event to break,

when he, at last, could be that sublimate
his body had aspired to, simply vapour
burning above a mound of ash.
But this would be a pyre to celebrate
his substance – words and pen and ink and paper
all the luminous trash

of magic and art. The conjuror could take
a parasol and out of it create
an ecosystem, or beneath
the parasol, meander in the wake
of *realpolitik* and contemplate
its dreadful colonnade of teeth.

His invented psyche was both male and female.
Two breasts had risen somewhere in his breast
like towers, so that when he took breath
two bodies rose and fell with it. His pale
shadow left the boy, the light caressed
his skin. He couldn't tell life from death.

He never was good company, would disappear
without one noticing and be discovered
wrapped in a blanket on the tramline
in the middle of the night. He never was there
and nowhere else. Everything he suffered
glowed in the language, turned to wine,

but such a wine as city children, bred
in stinking courtyards, would find in the street,
and when they drunk it, they would know
their nonsense validated by the dead.
He was the poet they'd queue up to meet,
in whose lost shadow they could grow.

In Memoriam István Vas
(1910-1991)

1

When your best friends are taken away,
when your mentor's daughter (forbidden,
you live with her in secret) dies of a tumour,
when you're constantly hiding
and the love of friends protects you
from starvation or bullets,
and you return by secret corridors
to Byzantium not Rome,
then you'll know at times of suspicion
that all is suspicious and everyone's done time,
and it's only the wind that blows
between words not through them
that constitutes poetry,
so you practise your craft
lightly, assiduously,
and when that world vanishes
you too take care to vanish
with the beauty and intimacy
of a secret friend, tumour or lover,
sensibly, quietlly, silently taking cover.

2

Candles in the window on All Souls' Day,
October wind gathering at the glass and rain
softening dead leaves. The tanks are rumbling again,
lorries are taking a whole town away.

We've been here before, whatever the season or year.
Your hesitant voice in mid-sentence, stopped in my ear.

Funeral Oration

The objects are on stage: their shadows link.
The sunlight turns the towel opposite
into the likeness of a man,
but the gallery is empty, on the brink
of someone's entrance. Empty chairs sit,
waiting. Someone draws a curtain.

Perhaps they'll step out and sit down. Perhaps
a child, more likely the blind woman who
has always lived here. The ledge
is hung with assorted greenery that drips
between the iron. Leaves bubble through
the railings. Somewhere there's a bridge

between the actor and his ghosts. A voice.
Some trick of speech. A broken window speaks
like tinkling glass, a bullet spits
into a cherub's puffed and vacant face.
Even the old rusted awnings creak
in chorus. Everything falls to bits,

the plaster and the stairs, the life within
the rooms, but one still steps out for a breath
of fresh air on the gallery.
It is as if he stepped out of his skin
or casually walked out of his death,
past the neat artillery

of railings, past the chairs, until he found
the one reserved for him, that had been waiting
like an open vowel
to close beneath him. And when the light turns round
you begin to see the human form, the sitting
figure hidden in the towel.

Two Rondeaux

1 *Unter den Linden*

In Unter den Linden and Wenceslas Square
the candles wink their *laissez-faire,*
people are trampling over borders,
packing their luggage. Cassette recorders
hiss like steam in the cold air,

cameras roll and spokesmen prepare
brief noncommittal statements, tear
pages from notebooks and wait for orders.
Prisons open: prisoners and warders
      mix in Unter den Linden.

In Prague and Budapest they wear
rosettes, wave flags. A furious year
gathers to a close. The wind disorders
ships of state and fleets of boarders.
Men link hands, dance and boldly stare
      across Unter den Linden.

2 *Clumsy Music*

A clumsy music: years lurch on
and fugitive clocks on the run
must settle debts by Hogmanay.
At Christmas guilty parents pay
the devil who pays debts to none.

Important things remain undone,
the boxes open: one by one
their ghosts are spirited away:
the piper stands by set to play
his clumsy music,

artificial yet homespun,
a rondeau much like this, begun
in hope as much as fear, to lay
his fears and keep wild hopes at bay
with dancing, linking hands, best done
to clumsy music.

Passenger

A long stop at a hot provincial station.
Heat turns to dirty water, little jewels
of smut, rivulets of perspiration.

The light crowds close, concentrates in pustules,
drops of poison, off-white, plump, opaque,
suspending grit in a soup of molecules.

The trees too are hemmed in. Their heads ache
in deserted railway yards, among lines
of empty wagons in sidings. They bake

in powders, asphalt heaps, among faded signs
announcing factories with broken windows,
wreathed in smears of smoke, in the confines

of yards with scatterings of scrap iron, rows
of used flasks abandoned years ago
to trucks blocking gates that neither open nor close.

*

The girl is far too smart. Her wrists are bare,
uncluttered. She wears four finger rings,
a thin gold anklet. How clean she is. Her hair

is neatly bobbed and shining. All her things
declare a certain distance: the delicate shoe,
the lycra top, the jet black pants' rustlings

and foldings. Even her scarlet nails look new.
But not her book, the *History of France*,
an ancient faded copy. She's half-way through

and turns each page with an impatient elegance.
Despite the carriage's wild jolts and swings
the book on her knee maintains its precarious balance
and this, as Holub tells us, gives her wings.

Transylvana

(for Peter Porter)

> 'Sylvan meant savage'
> W.H. AUDEN

*We're here to look for something, perhaps a house
buried half in the hill, with damp walls,
a jutting terrace and a long view across*

*the park to an artificial lake. Snow falls
on the branches and a surface of sheer ice
where a mob of skaters wheel and weave white petals*

*frilled with crystals, Transylvanian lace.
My mother's home town. The trees are thick with green.
Summer. Somewhere, in another place,*

*the skaters move to a frozen music between
the trees, performing a slow dance along the brink
of a precipice that cannot be seen*

*from where they are. They are lines of ink,
impossible to read now. A fountain jets
snow. The bandstand is a skating rink*

*full of toy soldiers. Above them the sun sets
and rises and sets again. My mother leans
on her elbows. Her brother pirouettes*

*across the lake. She is ill. A tree screens
the hidden steps which lead up to a hot
clear patch of sunlight. The ice queen*

*melts in a derelict house. A flowerpot
dangles dry stems in the porch. Where are we?
The skaters move in the distance, shot*

*through with dead light. Their translucency,
their quick black feet, remind me of birds.
The house says nothing, staring vacantly*

into the bushes. Above it vague herds
of clouds meander like soldiers on patrol
at a border station between two absurd

countries, watching empty wagons roll
up and down the track. The skaters rise
from the pond. Families stroll

among the trees. The fountain dries.
The city is full of unshaven faces
darting round corners, quick evasive eyes.

*

Our Virgil is thin. He waves a red carnation
in his outstretched hand. His mouth is sad.
Urine and darkness. Taxis hover at the station

like flies round rotten fruit. Roads being bad
we skate and bump along, juddering on scarred
cobbles, loose flakes of tarmac, past semi-clad

seventies blocks. The driver brakes hard
as we shimmy round a tight bend then lets fly.
Here only patience is its own reward

and patience is unending, numbing, sly,
deflated, almost anaesthetic in effect,
sensations slowing up, the batteries dry.

*

Virgil's wife is not long dead. He hankers
after her. Hence the obsessive tidiness.
Hence the old clothes queuing up on hangers,

a line of ghost wives, each in a different dress.
Hence the suitcases of old shoes, dead soles,
dead arches, metaphors of emptiness.

Waste not, want not. Words. Each word controls
a complex microsystem full of shoes.
There are housecoats, jackets, carefully packed rolls

of stockings, handkerchiefs. Someone might use
them sometime, these ritual cerements
whose buttons bless, whose broken straps accuse

the world–of–what–remains of innocence,
complicity, not knowing. The wardrobe
boxes up its knowledge, stores an intense

thickening, a denser universe. White globes
gather on shelves with the familiar stifling
smell of disease: bacteria, microbes, grubs.

*

Rainy mornings. Virgil unwraps a packet
of cheese, carefully slices it and lays
it out in a pattern. He is delicate

in his dealings. He fills whole days
with wrapping and unwrapping, making neat
divisions. He must go easy, paraphrase

the given grammar of each slab of meat
in simple sentences, short words, with stops
and dashes. He must become an aesthete

of necessity. In dark empty shops
he exercises taste, brings grace to bear
on grease, on cooking oil, thin chops.

*

Here are new apartments. Floors rise in austere
towers. The rubble remains: a long ditch
fills with rainwater the colour of flat beer.

Panels drop. The lift is stuck. This is a rich
country. It has silver, gold and bauxite,
natural gas, a seaboard. It can afford a hitch

or two, a twenty-watt bulb on a winter night,
a telephone exchange like a starved behemoth
straddling an unlit street. Basically it's all right:

you can have people or food but not both.
The building stutters, blunders to a stop.
The ditches breed defiance first, then sloth.

*

It's spring. Virgil negotiates the hill
above the city, steep, up crumbling steps
with a view out over spires, an idyll

from his childhood. An orange river creeps
below him, escaped from a paintbox and spilt
across brown paper. Beside it, small heaps

of rubble wait for houses never built.
They shrink to miniature pyramids
of powder. Sunlight reveals a soiled quilt

of roofs and walls. Cars scuttle like invalids
from block to block.
                          Enough of looking down,
of light stored patiently under the eyelids,

time to look up to the spectacular crown
of the city and the vast five star hotel
moated in mud, a petrified eiderdown

of cloud squarer than the rest, parallel
to the flat streets below, sheltering
its nightflown and exotic clientele

of representatives (who knows what they bring
or what they take away). It can't be much,
thinks Virgil and keeps clambering.

*

Virgil leads his visitors to the only
reliable eating place in town. He smiles
with sad sharp eyes, a smile both lonely

and endearing. High summer reconciles
hill, hotel and river in an embrace
of light. Light drips from guttering, from tiles,

pours down steps, down the green carapace
of copper domes, shimmers across bushes,
tucks itself into leaves, settles like lace

on last night's puddles and webs, rushes
down streets, bursts round corners in wild beams.
Busy times. The proprietress brings dishes

of soup specially prepared. The bowl steams.
A terrace with a tree. A cabin proclaims OASIS.
Cola labels. Plastic. The whole place dreams

of order, is a kind of synthesis.
Its cheap and easy kindnesses must prove
something to someone, provide a basis
for argument, a point from which to move.

*

*The ticket hall. Two bare bulbs burn. A third
has given up the ghost...Ghosts stand in queues
at holes. Ghosts bandy words*

*behind the counter. Successive greys infuse
a solid glass curtain. Beneath its waves two ghosts
engage in a discreet and aimless exchange of views.*

*

*The traffic lights too have given up. The dead
drive dangerously among the living. A policeman
flourishes his red stick like a neatly severed head.*

*

The trams have sagging bellies. They drag their heels.
They've eaten too much rust. It takes four men
to steer them straight with four bent steering wheels.

When soldier meets driver he makes a proposition.
When driver meets soldier he makes a contribution
thereby maintaining both in honest apposition.

Two old men meet. They shake hands. One has lost
a leg. Friends of different tribes, they speak
the ruling language. One waits till the other has crossed

the road before moving back into his own ethnic
group. The other hobbles on, part of the great
majority; amiable and sick.

*

When patient meets doctor an envelope
passes betmeen them. One offers obols
or collateral, the other offers hope.

*

The central square. The statue of the just
king (old dispensation). About him six
flags of the new salute in a strong gust.

The tiny local leader (new dispensation) kicks
his hind legs up, lets fly a leader's fart.
The old leader once kicked against the pricks:

the rough provincial redefines his art.

*

Virgil has friends. His contemporaries
remember everything, keep each other alive.
Everyone has his or her list of stories.

So does everyone else. People arrive
at individual outstations and make their peace
with consciences, authorities. They survive

as long as possible. Their numbers decrease,
their books smell ever damper, their pictures fade.
Some die on operating tables. Some piece-

meal, by stages, head downward, their bills unpaid,
their buttons undone. One falls under a train
after a drop too much, one having made

her bed and put on nightclothes. Their pain
is stored in umbrellas, overcoats, magazines
with half-solved puzzles. It remains

to be tidied up. Tidiness means
control and end. The pernickety
scuttling, the counting out of spoons,

the final indispensible dignity.

Virgil's Georgics

(after the illustrated calendar of Béla Gy. Szabó)

January

Moonglow. Night. Ice cold.
Trees furred like bears.
The stars have cold hard eyes.
And so have bears.

February

A frightened rabbit sprints across a field.
A frosty creature, half bat, half bear,
clings to a tree. Small flowers of frost
explode in bushes, splinter in the air.

March

A woodpecker. Trees tangled.
A nail scratching on glass.
Frozen hair on a dead man.
Shadows like soft claws.

April

A narrow ambitious branch. A bud in swell.
A herb garden. A chestnut tree. Birds unroll
across the sky. In 1954
I could put my arms around the bole.

May

Poplars full of thrushes. Sky leans
on earth. The river dreams.
Shrubs light their torches. A bullfinch
sputters on a branch, bursts into flames.

June

The cuckoo counts your years. An oil green shade.
The grass sports asterisks and nipples.
The lean black water on the pond traversed
by indolent white ripples.

July

The lake steams. Grebes cackle. A distant shower.
Star responds to star. Black clumps dither
under trees in an electric storm. Thunder.
Lightning. Changeable weather.

August

A grasshopper swings absent-mindedly.
Few days left to swing.
One sharp beam of sunlight is enough
to burn his wing.

September

On my first day at school my mother cried
but I whistled at my schoolfellows.
Around my feet the dead leaves
were dancing like swallows.

October

A leaf rattles. A bough lies on the ground
like a lost umbrella. A live branch groans
under the chattering rain and feels
a sharp ache in its bones.

November

A magpie among aspens. All things
curve in on themselves, aware
of what is still to come:
province of bat and bear.

December

A TV frost. Interference. A snowflake
breaks up in a scraggy oak.
All things given over to destruction.
A gun. A joke.

Romanian Brown

(for Irina Horea)

Political crises, shortages, rising crime.
The dictator's palace is unwittingly postmodern.
Life proceeds under the now-benign, now-stern
paternal gaze of Freudian Father Time.

If looks could kill...In high-rise flats the click
of keyboards. The gentle sea-sigh of computers:
fingertips of neighbouring literatures
touch across the corpse of the body politic.

Editors and translators conspire in the cold.
A chill runs down those delicate hands.
The TV spouts videos, foreign rock bands:
nothing now can ever again grow old.

Beggars are drifting through deserted squares
like paper sacks or ghosts of dancing bears.

*

Under the eyes a deep raw umber opens
into the warmth of the self like a letting-go,
and one slides through it to the marrow
in the thigh-bone and the thick translucent lens

of the joints. It is as strange as the world;
as disturbing in its brilliant intimacy
as the metaphor of the heart, that literary
device; as odd as the drowned sailor's pearled

and erotic eyes; as peculiar as the voice
you hear when you speak. No one who lives
in ordinary rooms with the great imperatives
of work and need lives there entirely by choice.

To sit in the dark settees of the eye is to know
the heart as literature, to suffer and let go.

*

Warm greys and browns. The softer certainties
assume jumpers and skirts, melt into tights.
The world must be civilised. Each colour invites
a cool intimacy between intelligent entities.

Long spatulate fingers stretch across a web
of nerves cocooning the fly of desire
which must nourish us somehow. But we tire
of its endless demands and night too starts to ebb.

The night is dark as coffee. The bushes outside
move in the wind, both hot and cold at once.
The trees are tossing their heads with impatience
and the whole sky begins suddenly to slide.

A kind of desperation runs through the deep
brown of the eyes and judders into sleep.

*

Solitary climbers sleeping at the tense
edge of precipitous forests under a dark brown
shower of needles stolidly arrowing down
into the earth can feel a bear's presence

(there are still bears in Europe, and wolves too)
in the soft pad and roll of the wind as it treads
towards them. The early autumn sheds
furred leaves which gradually form a thick glue

and a bird sings on the sharp snow-covered peak.
A woman lies in her tent, her dark brown hair
spread beneath her like the claws of a bear,
and all the bears and wolves begin to speak.

In a clear glass of Irish whiskey a train
pulls away from the platform through dawn rain.

*

A deep smudge of brown, something like a forest,
suggests an entrance into a possible past.
The dead come and go there like the forgotten caste
of an old religion. A woman offers her breast

to someone frail or a wolf or some kind of bird
in a potent act of charity or witchcraft.
The leaves are shivering in a delicate draught
between the pages of a book, hidden under a word.

Someone is saying: *Nature is your mother
and father* and points to a hole in the ground.
Lips meet lips with a distant sucking sound
and the hair rises, soft as a pigeon's feather.

Magic is suspect. An ancient figure stumps
between two sets of rusted petrol pumps.

*

The cloacal anteroom of the railway station. Pale
urinal yellows of the early morning.
The whole country disappears without warning
swallowed by night. The dark begins to fail.

But to think, and think...and now thin lines of steam
creep through the compartment, unfurl in grey,
briefly compose themselves before fading away.
The trains are coupling in a wet dream.

The bears are here too. They lumber across the track
in their furred overcoats. I watch them sadly.
I put out my hand to them. I know how badly
I need them. And look, they are calling me back.

And then I drift awake. And soon we start.
The train shakes like a tremor in the heart.

*

Blown like faint dust into the universe
whose eyes are both distant and close, this nagging pain
accompanies the sensation of being home again
as if one's own life were running in reverse.

Backwards into youth, backwards into childhood, back
into something formless yet vital, a directionless force
that stirs and disturbs. Somewhere a rocking horse
rises and dips, mouth grimaces then grows slack,

relaxing into a satisfied droop of the lips.
It doesn't last. The dust is whirling up a storm
desperate for affection, the remembered form
of the reaching hand as it grasps the bar and grips.

Raw umber, the rawer the better. The wood
receives you with its unfathomable good.

The First, Second, Third and Fourth Circles

1

Most cities approximate to a circle and so does this,
curled about the double bend of its river, on one side snuggling
to cliffs and hills where the cool air shuffles through a park with
       cedars,
a cogwheeled railway, a deserted tram stop,
some concrete tables for ping-pong or for chess,
and benches where migrant workers from Romania
sleep to shave in the morning by a working fountain,
hearing at night the wind in its mild cups
stumble up stairs between gardens, trailing a cloak
of lightbulbs and shopsigns over the gentler slopes
which are peopled with villas and baroque excrescences,
belvederes, weathervanes, cherubs and furies, cupolas and turrets,
a wrought-iron gate with doorbells and nameplates
which allows a visiting wind to drift through the hallway
between two apartments whose front doors give on to
large Ottoman carpets and rugs hung on walls,
and endless shelves of once-subsidised literature,
to say nothing of rattling East German spin driers,
expressionist plumbing and between-the-wars pictures
such as are found even in bedrooms of fifties estates
where no one's disturbed except for the sheepdog
slumped on a doormat, listening to its owners
snoring aloud in partitioned compartments
stuffed with old furniture intended for bigger rooms,
or howling to late cars or the crumbling glass
shattered on the high street where two drunks are fighting
and the police pick up girls from discos just for the hell of it,
doing handbrake turns by domed Turkish baths
sweeping down the embankment, past the olympic pool,
the chain-store installed in a reconditioned cellar,
the emptying restaurant with tables in the yard
where a few stray napkins float between chairlegs
in this mildest of weathers down in the square
or up at the museum-palace with its soaring prospects
and prancing statues of princes pulling faces
at the black of the night-time Danube, surveying the far side.

2

Cars are creeping round the portico of the Prussian style Academy,
the Westminster gothic of Parliament and the fifties modernist
White House of what was just a few years ago
the party headquarters, and beyond it the boulevard,
Angelfield, New Pest, and the distant industrial suburbs
beyond the third of the ring roads, the third arc shielding the second,
and the second haunting the contours of old city walls
embedded in tenements of the innermost ring,
pierced by radial highways, cafés, department stores.

3

Nineteenth-century grid-maps where everyone lives
but wants to move out of, in one room or two rooms
or one and a half-rooms, ranged about the communal courtyard,
the sound of a tap or a radio, a beggar or busker,
under the residents' own square of sky, towards which climb
neglected stairs with blown away putti,
untrustworthy lift-shafts which back in the dark days
brought terror to everyone, when in the dawn hours
the lift started up and a car was seen at the entrance,
and a single shepherded figure disappeared off the grid-map
into uncharted country beyond the reach of the suburbs.

4

The local girls are offering rides in a handy apartment
to the accompaniment perhaps of a video,
while next door, behind secessionist doors,
the lecturer types out his lecture and the German quiz host
slides down a cable which the whole block has paid for
and a lost voice interrogates itself at the mirror
or sips from its little black cup of resentments
which keep the heart beating all through the night.

The Lost Money

I'm lying down flat on the floor just reading
when the money starts to fall out of my pocket,
not merely money – keys and tickets, shreds
of paper handkerchiefs – but it's the money
that appears most real, and I keep thinking
my pockets are not deep enough because it trickles
through my fingers even through the cloth,
and I remember or redream the time
a pickpocket once in the Tuileries
slipped her hand into my pocket and I
grabbed at it, her scrawny wrist
a fish fresh out of water, the coins like scales
spilling from my pocket till I wake.

If it comes to that I guess I've never known
the value of cash, unlike my parents,
one of whom was paid in lard, the other
perhaps in salt, I can't remember which,
and they were anxious that I might go hungry,
which was annoying then, particularly
since I felt guilty, having made them worry
about having to go and get more money,
and here I am at forty, vaguely aware
of something slipping from my pocket, a dream
or dreams which feel too much like cash,
but go on reading, gathering up loose change
and thinking it's all right and still not worrying.

Unlike I suppose the pair that I keep seeing
drifting about town. Let me describe them to you.
The man has a beard and lurches violently
from one place to another. His beard is short,
his face square. While she stands at the bus stop
in apparent indifference, he gets down on his knees
and peers between her legs, from front, from rear.
She stands unmoving, looks away. He lurches
again, growls at a passing woman, mutters,
then resumes his work. The bus arrives. He sways
on to the platform. She turns round, her cut lip
and bulging eye immobile, follows him.

Next time she stands before the subway entrance
and he appears behind a pillar, beckons,
and she starts to walk in his direction.
Her trousers are striped, her jumper a dull yellow.
In the nearby block a woman takes a dirt tray
down to the chute marked RUBBISH
and discovers a human couple in the primal
position. Darkness. A hasty pardon.
She withdraws. When he does, it is to piss
into the chute and when the pair pack up
they pass into the street, continue their game
of follow-my-leader. Her cheeks are heavy, swollen,
shining, faintly blue, her bruised lips bear
a faint glaze of saliva which disturbs me
as if loose change were spilling from her mouth.

Variations on Radnóti: Postcards 1989

1

A wicked cherub perched on a pilaster
(His torso only) portending disaster
In somebody's gateway.
He grins and winks: half menace, half play.

2

The bustiest blonde in town some six yards high
who smirks behind sunglasses on a fire-wall
advertising the state lottery, may be a spy
but is in any case far from impartial.
If only I could squeeze her mammoth four-foot tits
I too might manage on state benefits.

3

Mother and child on a balcony.
Behind them the river stirs and shifts.
Parliament looks on and creaks
down delicate buttresses and broken lifts.

4

The miracle of the statue's foot which leaks
medicinal water. The miracle of the boutiques.
The miracle of *wirtschaftswunder*. But now we are
talking one miracle too far.

5

This is more like it, a balding middle-aged man
feet firmly planted, a mild pot belly, dressed
in quasi-military gear;
in his hand a peaked cap and a thirty-year plan
to confound both east and west,
give or take a year.

Black as in Coffee

The way the spoon almost stands up. The way
the tiny cup fits into your palm, like
an amulet of darkness in broad day-
light. The way it is still as a lake
in blackest Lilliput.
                              There is in Europe
a kind of vacancy this fills, as it now fills
my own, in one black concentrated drop
as my internal barometer falls.

In the centre of the centre, at the core
of the pupil, there is a line that leads
to the centre of the heart, a tiny pool

for the last moon to sink into. There's more
of the world than this, we know, though little beads
of darkness gather there. But that's OK. That's cool.

The Looking-Glass Dictionary
(for Gabriel Fitzmaurice)

1

Words withheld. Words loosed in angry swarms.
An otherness. The whole universe was
other, a sum of indeterminate forms
in motion. Who knows what the neighbour does
behind closed doors? You hear the chime
of the doorbell, the faint mechanical
music of the radio. It's supper time.
A window opens on a cry or chuckle,
the rest is half withheld – should it be loosed
the window's quickly shut, the door slammed tight
to seal words in. Guessed at or deduced
darkness arrives feathering words with night.
There they grow wings, like owls and nightingales,
screeching or singing till their meaning stales.

2

Screeching or singing till its meaning stales,
the cold grey light has drawn you from your bed,
the words go scuttling homeward, their bright tails
between their legs and shelter in your head.
The airport. Night. December. Rough and grey,
a blanket covers you. The windows snore
half-way between dust and snow. The day,
trying to raise itself, creeps under the door
and offers you a cup of tea. Its alien milk
enters your bloodstream like the wizened face
of the old woman with her tray. That silk
ribbon of liquid confirms your sense of place,
and winds you in, a line that anchors, warms,
and lets you enter its own world of forms.

3

They let you enter their strange world of forms
out in the playground, on the rough brick wall
where they have left their messages in storms
of chalk and paint. Their distances still call
for you, back in the classroom or a street
at some resort where you once spent the summer
among arcades, to the rock and roll beat
of neon lights, and further out and dimmer,
a buoy blinking through foggy yellow air
or the gentle drone of cricket commentary
in daytime heat which wraps you in blonde hair
and scent of oil, then dies in memory,
hovering in a haze before it fails,
like faint vibrations down deserted rails.

4

Faint vibrations of trains along the rails:
where are we now? Abroad again or home?
Between two kinds of sound. Their echo trails
along behind you (words themselves won't come.)
What did your mother say before you woke
to this? Her ribs vibrated with the thrum
of inner traffic. Something like a croak
surfaced at your throat and the hot drum
of her heartbeat made your heart dance. The slow
pulse of her blood blubbed and retreated, drove
your tongue before it with its enormous O,
and educated you to the word 'love'.
Like all words that apply and predicate
desire and loss, it brooked of no debate.

5

Desire and loss do not permit debate.
Where do the inner journeys go? They end
in trails of words, a kind of nonsense state
you cannot trust. And true, it is no friend
to kindness or reason. Words were treacherous.
Do you remember how at school they made
you catch the worms you would dissect? The fuss
as they wriggled and stiffened in formaldehyde?
The Latin names that crystallised that weak
mulch of muscle? The humours of the eye
that wept and spurted a transparent streak
of laughter between a language and a cry?
The Queen's English wrapped the pain in sound
that was articulate, in which the pain was drowned.

6

Articulate, you know how pain is drowned
and resurrected, undergoes baptism
and dies once more. The vessel runs aground
time and time again, drawn to the bosom
that nourished it. First time I saw the sea
was in December at Westgate. Huge grey jaws
snapped at the rocks, the white seethed in fury
like a pan full of fat, but cold. One word draws
the sea up, another repels it. We met
in a hut on the cliff-top, cub scouts with string
and diagrams of knots. The faint sun set
on the horizon. We were children playing
with water pistols. Food appeared on the plate
like clockwork and the clock did not run late.

7

But clockwork sometimes runs down or runs late.
The words my mother spoke were rarely home
to her, or moved at another, slower rate
which could not follow her. Somehow the room
was never hers. When she was cross, her eyes
ran before language, even before her voice,
which issued from a deep, raw, oversize
mouth inside her. We knew she had no choice,
that it would be all kindness, kisses, tears.
After the terrors (the camp, the deaths, the strange
sexual crudeness) we knew that what appears
is merely a sign and yields life little change,
that mum was a sea that ran your ship aground,
her voice a channel for that kind of sound.

8

A narrow channel. Now the empty sound
of a ship's engine, now a soft gull peeling
from the clouds, a bruise or an old wound,
plaster cracked across the bedroom ceiling.
The ceiling rose opens in a brilliant blur
and the bulb in the rose expands in purple
echoes of itself. The rain is damp fur
on the window. Your bedclothes ripple
in the night tide as you swim the sudden dark.
Your parents' voices merge with traffic. They
are arguing. Their harsh words leave no mark
but fade into the dream of every day.
The clock goes ticking on but your life runs
straight down the hill of poetry and puns.

9

Most poetry runs down the hill of puns –
that is what makes it treacherous and yet
so utterly persuasive. Mothers and sons
can mumble ambiguities and let
that rich thick soup of meaning nourish them.
The language outside meets the ur-language within
with the consistency of dream
which sits like a faint moisture on the skin.
My father's voice. A gentle coaxing lost
in the depths of his chest. His musculature
is iron swelling in his arms. Thin frost
covers him in a Russian forest. Pure
narrative lines run through him. He stands
in the street with the city in his hands.

10

Out in the street, the city in his hands,
he crosses and recrosses, hard at work.
He builds his tongue of vowels and consonants
with ifs and buts, emerging from the murk
of winter. He gathers them up like notes
shuffled through the cold hands of the dead
who smile at us from under heavy coats
of dust and snow. The coins bear his own head
as guarantee. We're at a football match
above the river. The Brylcreemed players race
about the pitch in baggy shorts. We watch
the old men on the terraces. I see his face
darkening as we walk home. The light runs
along his arm which could be anyone's.

11

His arms and mine, both could be anyone's.
We're only bodies, bodies are what we have.
We float in them among the crowd in patterns
down the tidal street towards the grave
caverns of the tube. We are a small cell
in the organism which encloses us,
lost travellers, a tiny human smell
that thickens when we rise, like Lazarus,
spectral and intimate and normal, home
among the words that mean us and reflect
our faces and possessions. We are the Rome
that all roads lead to, the dense idiolect
of heavens where we sleep and wake. It stands
in the world, half Hungary's, half England's.

12

This tiny world, part Hungary, part England,
is the macaronic my parents speak –
my dad especially. There is no bland
unbroken stream. The words seem to leak
in drips, wearing away all sensible matter,
making minute impressions, exhausting them.
I see this and am lost in multicoloured chatter
that seems to spread and deepen: spit and phlegm
and croak and fricative whose sounds mean me
and everything that can be concentrated
into the me I vaguely sense, that free-
standing monument, marble and gold-plated,
sole owner of my lexical demesne
of spotless glass where words may sit and preen.

13

A spotless glass where anyone may preen
when it is dark outside, the window throws
your image back at you. Who is the unseen
and uninvited guest in your dumb shows?
Only the skin – hands, legs, face – remain
hanging against the house opposite. Hair
disappears, clothes vanish. And now the rain
jewels and fractures till you're hardly there.
Trying to say 'you' to those smears of light
seems inappropriate. Recall the face
of your mother, that hollowed out, tight
mask in the photograph, almost a grimace
in forty-five? It creeps under the screen
of language, blankly refuses to mean.

14

The language here blankly refuses to mean
what it's supposed to. The signs are lost.
If you could only read the space between
or babble in fiery tongues at Pentecost.
What's gone is gone. Parents might be the first
to vanish but children soon follow. The winter sun
flashes off snow and the icy trees burst
with light. The world is what cannot be undone
nor would you wish to undo it when it speaks
so eloquently out of its dumbness, when
its enormous treasury of hours and days and weeks
resolves to this sense of now and never again.
It comes at you now in syllabic storms,
the words withheld then loosed in angry swarms.

15

Words withheld. Words loosed in angry swarms,
screeching or singing till their meaning stales
have let you enter their strange world of forms
like faint vibrations down deserted rails.
Desire and loss do not permit debate:
articulate, you know how pain is drowned.
You slept in beds when day was never late,
your voice a channel for the kind of sound
that rolls downhill in poetry and puns.
Out in the street, the city in your hands
lays down its arms, which might be anyone's –
Hungary, England are verbal shadowlands
of spotless glass where all may sit and preen,
blank languages whose words refuse to mean.

Travel Book

(for Anne Stevenson)

1

The ego grinds and grates like a machine.
The voyage out begins in classrooms where
stout boys in dirty tracksuits measure clean
ruled sheets of paper to a helpless stare
which pierces the heart. The teacher croons
like a pigeon, her words a soft cloud
full of light. The boys' faces are balloons
that drift below her, a bobbing crowd
of stupid gentleness. This one smells of shoes
and mud. His fingers clench and unclench,
his hair a lank mess. He did not choose
his head or body. The beginnings of a stench.
His nose runs. His nails have been bitten
down to a tiny slip on which nothing can be written.

2

Look. On this tiny slip of paper is written
the name of a plain woman. The thick lens
of her heavy glasses seems to fatten
her eyelashes to strokes made by blunt pens.
Her name is *kindness* and *friendship* and *you
will never know*. Indeed, how could you know.
Later you watch her feeling her way through
her dusty hall. This is how the blind go
into the world, resenting its bulk, annoyed
by its ill manners, its crude mischief. To live
by touch reminds lovers of the void
between beauty and desire. Can she forgive
her dead husband, her visitors, all the unseen
nonsense her eyes feed on? What does it mean?

3

We feed on nonsense whatever it may mean.
A polished grand piano butterflies
across the room, billows across the clean
floor, over the stove which crackles and sighs,
and settles by the window. Dark brown gloss
covers the eyes of Mr Shane, violinist,
now worn quite smooth, his moustache a light moss
under his polished nose. His slender wrist
is almost feminine. Art has no gender,
is an uneasy comfort zone where the mad
briefly settle and the sane diminish in wonder
at their predicament, which is a sad
and brilliant obsessession with pattern,
both raw and cooked, so soft and yet hard bitten.

4

The self cooked through is soft and yet hard-bitten.
Two tiny flirtatious girls in the back room
of a photographer's flat seem to be wrapped in cotton-
wool. An air of sentimental gloom
haunts the refugee party. I touch the hand
of the elder one: the current lifts me from
my low seat. At nine, I cannot understand
what's going on. I know there is a bomb
ticking in her flesh. Years later I find out
her dad takes saucy pictures for calendars.
The younger one bursts into tears. There is a shout
in the street that rises above the growling of cars.
One understands that sex is nothing new.
The mirror is no censor but tells you who is who.

5

What does the mirror say to the censor? Who
else can you talk to? One good friend steals
your father's stamps. Another tells you
the secrets of his parents' bedroom. It feels
odd being in a world like this. You pretend
to be handsomer than you are. Jealous
of others' success you invent a girlfriend
who helps you develop your sense of the ridiculous.
Being what you are you value romance
above sex but cannot help your hormones.
You accompany your frail ego to the school dance.
The Christmas chill enters your bones
with a special, undisguised, personal tenderness
that creeps and cools, erasing self in the process.

6

Talk like this erases self in process.
But what is self? Here are the beauties of night:
Angela, deep voiced; white-socked Brenda; Diana, no less
dangerous; Carol delicate. All of them bite
with rejection. Rejection is the law
of late childhood. Now you should sing
the beautiful teachers who filled you with awe,
of whose lessons you remember nothing
but the transcendence of their look
as it fluttered here and there, who could not reject
because their job was not to. The text book
bears witness to their names. The high elect
drift in their cold empyrean, a vacant blue
out of your range, that seems both valid and true.

7

But how do you know what is valid or true
when there is no sense of being, no fixed space
to move in, no vantage point or overview?
You don't know if the world's a human place
or some robotic jamboree in which
you yourself must appear with appropriate mask.
Weakness is your only guide, that faint twitch
behind the eyes when you are moved to ask
the necessary question. Your father's eyes,
a fat woman struggling through the rain,
an awkward delicacy under the disguise
of the poised girl, that hard-to-explain
vulnerability of the big man, the lost distress
of the body in the mirror as it sees itself undress.

8

What do you see at night when you undress,
when the conscious mask slips between one breath
and another only to slip back on? A game of chess
played by some adolescent knight with a filmic Death?
The Bergmanesque Grim Reaper? The Old Foe?
The photograph of a youthful father? The flounce
of a dress your mother once wore? Under the slow
moment, the immediate, quick, once and once
only sense of transition. The shop girl's shaking
hand as she pecks at the till. The brief smile
on the bus conductor's face as he is taking
your fare. Scrawled intercessions in the aisle
of the local church – those pregnant lines –
graffiti in the public toilets, signs.

9

Graffiti in the toilets, torn-down signs
at junctions. The Baptist minister glares
from his pulpit. Nearby, South Yorkshire mines
disgorge father and son. A teacher prepares
the next day's lesson. Peter Sutcliffe stalks
through Harehills and Chapeltown. In the pub,
girls in short leather skirts return from walks
down sidestreets, grab a spot of grub
and watch dominoes being slammed down hard
on marble tabletops. The whole world is
a dangerous romance, slowly edging forward
in the shadows, relying on memories
to get through its nightmares, meeting day
with the help of cigarettes, and cold pie on a tray.

10

Here is the ashtray's chaos, crumbs on a tray,
an empty glass. The blunt Northern accent
carries masculine warmth even in the grey
livery of garage and tenement.
Closed vowels, a rumbling in the belly.
Out on the moors harsher vowels of wind.
Spartan interiors. A sofa. The telly
by the wall. Down broken wet cobbles, blind
gropings of grass and weed. The poet in his chair
reciting Pope and Desnos. Children run
across a derelict site into a space that is nowhere
but must do. The city has room for everyone.
It does, after all, provide a kind of home:
crumbs on a tin tray, hair left in the comb.

11

Up-ended lead type, hair left in old combs:
lovers of small numbers go benignly potty;
big number men construct spectacular domes
and make long speeches. All is vanity
saith the preacher. A silver-headed man
labours among statues and word processors
turning language into an ingenious plan
to contain the universe and all its professors.
Why stop at the universe? My father picks
a stamp up with his tweezers and consults
his Stanley Gibbons. The world is full of maniacs
who hoard lost masterpieces in hidden vaults.
My mother vents her furies. The dictator resigns
after a fever, retires to a space between the lines.

12

After a fever, space between the lines
grows more attractive. Here the brittle hide
from gross events. A dazzling sun reclines
among the petals on the sill. Inside,
the cat pads across armchairs, a late fly
settles on the lampshade, the radio sings
to itself for ever and footsteps hurry by
without stopping. What continually brings
you up short? Your children trailing soft
fingers across the keyboard make their brief
excuses. Soon nothing substantial is left
except the words which offer no relief
from the bright precarious tedium of play
you read in negative at the end of the day.

13

You read in negative. At the end of the day
the light falls directly on you. Moon warms your skin
into endearments. My darling, you say
to the body whose pools you have swum in.
My dear. She catches a little moonlight
on her cheek and her shoulder. Now she dreams
of flying to her sick father, that shrunken, slight
figure in a distant bed. She moves through streams
of cloud and melts into sleep. The visitors
arrive with their negative gifts: the lamp
that glows black, cold fire, the open doors
of a closed room. It's hot in bed. She's damp
but cool – your life expands to fill the room
till there's nowhere to go. Come hope. Come home.

14

The question is where you go. Come hope, come home.
Her skin is palimpsest. You cannot read
her mind though you see it. At night, you roam
through the house watching the curtains bleed
to the floor. She is everything that holds
the pictures up, prevents headache, and turns
the world to language, sifting through the folds
of some larger brain, burning as fire burns
till you emerge like Tamino into music.
You try the word 'love', whisper 'death', and make
faces at yourself. You are growing sick
of eloquence. Perhaps you are beginning to awake
from the sleep of reason or are caught between
the teeth of words that grind like a machine.

15

The ego grinds and grates like a machine
producing tiny slips on which is written
the nonsense it feeds upon. What does it mean
to be a self, so soft and yet hard bitten?
What does the mirror say to the censor? Who
talks like this, erasing self in the process?
How do you know if it's valid or true?
What do you see at night when you undress?
Graffiti in the public toilets, signs
in the ashtray's chaos, pie on a tray
of upended type, hair left in the comb
after a fever, the space between lines
you read in negative at the end of the day.
The question is where you go. Come hope. Come home.

Portrait of My Father in an English Landscape
(for Peter Scupham)

1

The classic shot of my father is the one
in which he carries my brother in his arms
with me striding beside him, holding on
to his trousers. The past continually warms
the present. The nostalgia gap
is a pit into which images can fall
and never rise. Best to suspect a trap.
Yet there is something solid and spherical
about the figure I feel I have to build
into and out of language. He exhales
his own monument which hangs there, stilled
as the light which holds him but fails
to preserve the cells of wind that whistle through him
and could destroy his body at a whim.

2

Easy to destroy a body. A historical whim
drops him into childhood among white beards
and piety. There he stands, forever slim
and vulnerable, entranced by old men's words.
He waits at the foot of the bed. Tales and jokes,
small beaky women. Parables and sweets.
How did Jesus get to be God? Women stroke
his dark hair. His grandmother always greets
the returning schoolboy with a small gâteau.
An uncle draws a bag of squashed éclairs
from his pocket. Outside, big winds blow
up a storm. The world of tables and chairs
will never know what hit it. Soon they are gone,
preserved elsewhere but not worth sitting on.

3

Preserves and cakes. Eventually time sits on
the lot. Grandad got run down by a tram
and yet survived to claim the insurance. One
uncle opened a music shop. It closed like a clam
about him. The second grandfather died,
cancerous, still telling stories. The little beaks
are pecking in the kitchen. They provide.
There was a brother once among the relics,
a home child, insignificant, a paradox,
who died when a hill of sand came down
and covered him as he was playing beside the rail tracks.
He had a name too, a genuine proper noun.
Short words. God's scattered text. The scholar's passim.
Even on clear nights certain stars look dim.

4

On clear winter nights when even the dim
stars interject splinters of blue ice
into the conversation, dead faces swim
through wisps of cloud. Dante's paradise
glows in bright rings around the moon. There is rank
and order in their passage. Or so they say.
Ghost stories, gothic tales. A hostile tank
rumbles across the city and levels the way
to disjunction. My father in the office.
My father in the factory. In the road
with a lavatory pan on his head. His surface
is a broken narrative. He must load
his possessions onto the conveyor belt
of particularities, hard luck and guilt.

5

Particularities, hard luck and guilt
compose him. Mention his patience too,
also his kindness. His eyes are a warm quilt
to hide beneath. You can wander through
his fingers as through a wood (though similes
are not his style). You see a short man
full in the chest, thin legs, large nosed. He sees
the likeness, suspecting metaphor, can
marshal facts, add a column of figures,
size up a problem and suggest solutions.
All fathers are Prospero or else beggars
without authority. There are fashions
in viziers as in haircuts. His alchemical head
radiates a thin light which must be interpreted.

6

By what light though can he be interpreted?
He is the history I stand on with one leg.
I'm trying to peer into the murk and shed
light on my own behalf. Must Prospero beg
for interpreters? Listen, he is playing
his mouth organ in the forest. Others hum
or search for words. Something is weighing
on them. The icy wind has made them numb.
Soldiers without insignia, dying slaves
out of Michelangelo, they learn the tunes
appropriate to their sad huts and lost enclaves.
Their families are telling fortunes
in safe houses and ghettoes others have built
into chains of command, their bones cracked, blood spilt.

7

Chains of command crack bones. The blood spilt
underwrites him. One day his friends stole
a supply train. A true tale on a single stilt,
another terrifying anecdote to roll
towards posterity. One of many. What hurts
is the truth of every story, things being just
as they are, true without consequence, bit parts
in a ridiculous epic of cinematic dust.
Escape on the March Back. The First Sight
of the Chaotic Russian Army as they Spin
across Half Europe, mad Flight, sane Flight,
the Toiling Masses, Rape, Rapine and Repin.
Malenky robot. Three soldiers in a bed,
the woman beneath them crippled, maybe dead.

8

A woman crippled if not exactly dead
(his wife, my mother) offers him her cage
and he walks in. He knows she has touched dread
with her bare fingers. There is a savage
untenanted domesticity I could not begin
to measure. The reader must devote
time to getting this right, develop a skin
too tender to feel the world as anecdote.
Time to detach oneself. An overweight
man with a hernia, bad short term memory,
and need for companionship. Such late
revenges. Executions too summary.
I tell it wrong like he does. It's wrong to laugh
in the presence of a ghost or photograph.

192

9

The presences – not ghosts, nor photographs –
are symbols through which we walk together.
Our bodies are being resolved into epitaphs.
Outside, snow is working itself into a lather
about nothing. Language slips, words slide
and take pratfalls. I cannot quite conjure
this robust presence. Anecdotes hide
the very thing they describe in their pure
linear fashion. You can only focus
on one part of the picture, the rest shifts.
Perhaps that shifting is the true locus.
Perhaps anecdotes are frozen snowdrifts
that catch the light just so, shapes blown
and surfeited, whose centre remains unknown.

10

Surfeit of snow, the core remains unknown.
A winter park. He drags us forward, up
a slight hill. Our toboggan slithers on
and we descend. Soft landings. Now we cup
the snow in our gloved hands. A snowball.
The bus bonnet steams in the cold. The city
is an ice palace, the main street a great hall
approaching the square. His proximity
is his presence. The nearness of it. The wolf
enters his lair and asks for hot tea. The stove
in the corner warms us. Habitat and self
merge into sleep. It is a treasure trove
you cannot rob. The jewel's in the safe.
The wolf is in his lair. The children laugh.

11

The wolf in his lair, children begin to laugh
at their own fear. Kind wolf in a world of wolves.
Has father met the wolf? Wolves are the stuff
of legend. Their harsh morality revolves
about old prohibitions. One year Dad fell
from the first storey of a building site. His green
face in the hospital bed was shrill as a bell.
Poor wolf in a world of traps. Again the clean
lines of anecdote. I remember how he stroked
my face. Not then. Some other time. Just once
he let fly at me, when he had been provoked.
I had upset my mother. I felt his palm bounce
off my cheek. This wolf bites. He stalks alone
down the high street. Old solitary. Dry bone.

12

The high street is full of loners. Dry bones
in shop doorways. Here come the essences
under their layers of skin and flesh. Vague groans
of bodies in movement. Their circumstances
are apalling. We are not wolves but sheep
in the fold, gentle baas against the vast sky.
I imagine my father lying down, asleep
in that interior shelter where children cry
so faintly one can hardly tell their low
whimper from the dull sobbing of the wind.
The facts of any life are as they are, just so,
and never to be counted, stars in the sequinned
darkness, coloured sand to be sifted through
and banded, their edges neither straight nor true.

13

Bands of colour, edges just out of true,
conjure the Isle of Wight. I'm barely ten
and going through a religious phase. The blue
sky is the eye of God. Now and again
that clear sight homes in on something bright
and imposing. The teacher leads a prayer
like warm milk whose capillaries trickle right
down into my socks. No fatherly care
can ever be as sweet as this. The universe
has gentle hands to cradle a child's face.
It has its off-days too when it issues terse
directives, when it stares blankly at the place
relief should come from. I watch dad chew
his dinner, address him casually as you.

14

My father eats. I call him casually. You.
We argue for the sake of it as always,
because it is natural to argue.
I'm impatient. Some mischievous devil plays
us off against each other at opposite ends
of the table. I hate my impatience, hate
the cause of it. So hard to make amends,
impossible perhaps. It's getting late,
I look at my watch. He makes that worried gesture
with his hands which moves me. His eyes
are a warm cave swimming in faint moisture,
now turned inward, now open in surprise.
They hang there when the anecdotes are done.
The classic shot of my father. That's the one.

15

The classic shot of my father is the one
most easy to destroy. Historical whim
preserves a secret well worth sitting on,
though even on clear nights its stars are dim
particularities of luck and guilt.
He is a light that must be interpreted
through chains of command, cracked bones and blood spilt,
through women crippled, and often left for dead.
A presence, like the ghost in a photograph,
a surfeit, a core that can't be truly known.
The wolf is in his lair. The children laugh
in the high street at the old loner with his bone
and bandana, his edges neither straight nor true.
Their father waits for them and calls them You.

The Lost Scouts

1

The caniculae are almost over. Cool
intermittent winds chase each other round
lush trees. Dead leaves are lying on the ground
and a light lace mantle descends on a pool
at the fag-end of the second millennium.

The wheels of the old world groan as they turn
over the bones of the dead who won't learn
their lessons and are destined to remain dumb.

The doors are open. The train empties
then fills, moves off. It is a great effort
moving towards the fire. The cog wheel railway
rises towards the woods' outer ring of darkness
without any visible means of support,
and time turns backwards into yesterday.

2

My father was a scout light years ago.
In a world of health and efficiency, he rowed
and hiked while the world was waiting to explode
under his feet, when those who could would blow
with it.

       He would leave the dark city down the river,
winding through valleys, up and down the scree-
paths of mountains in lung piercing clarity,
that could sustain a boy almost for ever.

Friends sang and played Baden-Powell games
in colonies of urban dust, wore ties
with toggles, khaki shorts and walking boots,
kept rank and discipline to funny names
adapted from wood-craft, moved through woods like spies
in a body cult of uniforms and suits.

3

They sing now, as they sang when there were many,
when the dead were young and wore vests and grins
and went diving and tramping: Mowglis, Sir Galahads,
Chingachcooks, Wolves, all of a mythical company
bound by codes and by magic, where manhood begins
with oaths and secrecy, discipline and parades.

And so they marched off, being Jews, to places
the century saved for them. Marched to the tunes
of the day that were sung in the cabaret and the beer hall,
their bodies still young but with premature faces,
my father, Akela, the wolf pack, to make their fortunes
among the lost behind a fence or a high wall,

fifty-five years ago along with their leadership,
their heroes and brothers as if on a day trip.

4

So history came and blew them apart. Their arms
and legs and heads flew off, their bodies aged
in camps. They froze in forests. Fires raged
in ovens at the heart of unbearable farms.

The handsomest, cleverest, most athletic…the fire
consumes whatever is thrown on it. Those once burned
remained burnt, but some, as always, returned
with only their whiskers singed while the flames leapt higher.

I have a photograph of six of them
straddling a fallen tree trunk. Only two
survived the time. Luck smuggled such through
prison gates, in some cases only *pro tem.*

But I can't help thinking of the lost scouts,
their songs, their chants, their ever more distant shouts.

5

Here they are now. My father among a hundred
lost boys, knights of the round table, the dark wood
glooming behind them, their faces turned red
by the central fire which signifies brotherhood.

Memory washes away the scent of ashes
and rounds off the sharp edge of broken glass,
but they keep the fire going with twigs and rushes
like decent schoolboys in a promising class.

Old men from Canada, Spain, The States, Australia,
with wives and children, gathered as if
for the Grand Order of Water Buffaloes
or the Rotary Club, wearing invisible regalia
of firelight as the night-cold clutches stiff
arthritic fingers and feels its arthritic toes.

6

They sing and tell stories. That is the role of the old
who have travelled the roads and rails of atrocity.
They sing old songs as they move through the city
in business suits, fully insured and bankrolled,
in laboratories, concert halls, cool studios,
high office blocks, respectable addresses,
their tears tucked under the pillowslips of brilliant successes
or sizzling in embers under long melted snows.

This language is too fancy for them. Let them crack jokes.
Let them remember old japes. Let them recall excursions
on the Danube or any other river. Let them have a drink
or two, let them over-eat and grow ulcers. Old blokes
with baseball caps, their peculiar foibles and aversions.
Old guys in their cups, in fine fettle, in the pink.

7

But as we leave the gardens of the hotel where the fire
dies down and move to the edge of the forest
a man begins screaming. It is now, the merest
moment, trapped in the moment, as if in some dire
prison. A single man in the wood, furious,
cursing invisible enemies, while our bus waits
like a dim lit room. There is something that hates
the world, it seems. The man in the wood is its curious
emanation.

       One of the scouts had made
a kind of a dummy he called the spirit of evil
and threw it on the fire where it fell with a long hiss.
It was a strange moment and I felt afraid
thinking of other fires, of the work of the devil
whatever that is. I prefer not to think of this...

8

What is better in early September than these
reliable trees closing over our garden
on the leafy side of the city? It is no great burden
carrying the memory of them. They please
me now, the next day, as they had the eyes
of boys my father's age before they grew
into their old age of returns. There's nothing new
in nature, not that you'd know, but the surprise
of complexity and light.

       The poet Radnóti, who died
in a ditch, wrote of his garden and his wife
on a summer afternoon drinking with his friends.

Then came history, and the wolfpacks they cried
appeared at the door and demanded their one life
and they gave it, like that, and so the evening ends.

Bruno Schultz in Amber: The Demons

There I was looking after Numero Uno,
a tiny cog in the wheels of commerce, just
a speck in the mirror eyeing a gorgeous bust.
I was like a character out of Bruno
Schultz, confined to bed, telling tall tales
of grandfathers and earwigs, with a tame
aesthetic protector to absolve me from all blame.
I can simply tell a joke if all else fails,
I thought, then remembered Schultz's fate, shot dead
in the street by a jealous officer of the Wehrmacht.
Perhaps I'd made my life up. Perhaps I'd stacked
a whole library in my empty head
and this was my life, or some of it, in print
on yellowed paper you might read at a squint.

The bed was like a page turned down. Out crept
a few demons of the conventional kind:
itches and burns, a verruca, undefined
scabs, weird discolourations, each adept
at its own mischief. A monastic scribe
might have depicted them fleeing city walls,
at the edge of the text, in shrivelled petals,
with the faces of a long forgotten tribe.
What insignificances had I given
birth to? Had they all conspired to haunt me?
One monster kept on multiplying, lost
in endless clones of itself. He'd never be driven
from my body, would always be there to daunt me
while I lay there like a child with fingers crossed.

The clothes hung on the door congealed to one
fat figure, somewhat like Sidney Greenstreet
in *The Maltese Falcon*. It was a discreet
appointment I had to make with him. I'd done
something wrong and he was to admonish
and threaten me in that lumbering way of his,
breathing and billowing in the impossible breeze.

Pointless hoping, however I might wish
for him to go. I was like Peter Lorre
but tinier still and much more vulnerable.
A bullet would find me ten minutes from the end.
I could almost hear my father begin to worry
about my lack of sleep. It meant more trouble:
a son to re-dream, one more thing to mend.

A Pink Face

1

I thought I had a sense of my own life
there in the hotel drawer, just underneath
the television, something I'd wear like a wreath
at my funeral to focus the world's grief
at my so precipitate passing at eighty-two
after a hearty meal. Perhaps I'd cut
my wrist and the blood had dried already, but
that's not how it felt at the time. Then, through
the hotel window, appeared a swollen face,
one of those stucco heads, filled out with flesh
of lurid pink, a slice of ham on a dish,
grinning violently. This was the wrong place
for such nightmares to appear. It could not last,
but I was scared and shut the window fast.

2

The pink head hung in the air, faintly burning
like a distant match. Below it the whole town
was going about its business, walking up and down,
entering doorways, setting forth, returning.
Boys were kicking a ball. A little girl
looked out of a window. At night three drunks
roared a popular song amid solid chunks
of fallen masonry. Leaves lifted in a swirl
of wind. Clouds sprinted over the rooftops
and the sun dodged in and out extremely fast
and bright. Time was doing its mad march past
in a parody of precision. The Keystone Cops
sat at the wheel and set off in pursuit.
The stucco head was slowly taking root.

3

Later I saw it again, leering through the grain
of the pine desk the hotel had provided
for visiting academics. There was something lop-sided
about the room. It seemed to fall like rain
and run away from me down through the sluice

of the street outside. Meanwhile the face composed
itself into a form of scrutiny, its eyes half closed,
the mouth set hard. It would accept no excuse,
however feasible, for my lack of sense
of life, and though I knew it was just statuary
I still felt guilty, scared and jittery
in its august, hallucinatory presence.
Whose face was it really? Out of what mould
had its features fallen, furious and cold?

4

Or was this merely fantasy, the kind you see
in architects' notebooks and harmless for all that?
The streets were full of them, curving from flat
and undemanding walls, peering through a tree
as people passed beneath. They wore the faces
of lost decades. If they had memories
they kept them hidden under the scuffed frieze
they rose above, grotesque old commonplaces
in a fallen language, a dog Latin *bow-wow*
while real life went on in the darkened rooms
they were set to guard, among the fading blooms
of floral wallpaper, surviving any old how
across the street, past curtains, in the crooks
of armchairs, in the smell of rotting books.

5

My paranoiac schizophrenic stage
was blooming nicely. Goodbye to the Me
defined by ancestors and society
(but there was no such thing). One self could rage
against another or completely ignore
its wild companions. Somebody once claimed
everyone had to be somewhere. I blamed
the world, that ticking thing outside the door
with its pink face. One day it would explode
and take me with it while the citizens
of my two countries got on with their lives
down million miles of straight and narrow road.
The self is a dead loss. The window opens
on a pale pink head. Something at least survives.

In the Cabbage Grove

The women are walking the cabbage grove
towards a loss they cannot comprehend.
 Quick simple tongues
will click and lips grow wet and spend
their moisture in a ritual of songs
  that pass for love.

They pass beside me, already lost
in shadow and the comprehensive night
 which like a hem
has swept them up, away. What light
perpetuates and mollycoddles them,
  and at what cost?

Admiring their strong legs, their skin
of crusted leather and their death in groves
 of cabbages,
I cannot speak but know their voices prove
the gruffness mine. They are the savages
  I gather in.

Daffodils

I am bothered by the nagging translucency
of these daffodil petals in their Busby Berkeley outfits
of six yellow skirts around a frilled bell
darkening to its centre, their stern stalks bunched
in the glass on the sill by a warm brown wall,

and I'm wondering if I can make any sense of daffodils
(or Diaphenias or Daffy Ducks for that matter)
or of any of that unwonted clutter of names
which has done nothing to force them into flower
quite in the way they do here or to gather

those pleated petals to such concord of dancing
or stillness, recalling the skin of my mother
at fifty, slouched, puckered and dying,
her flame indrawn under bruised plums and purples,
or my skin, for instance, in its cold variations

on one theme of pink, full of cracking and byways
that grasp at the sunlight, almost transparent,
opening on something that passes them by
or cuts a swathe through them, not quite the sun,
but having the nonchalance of sunlight.

Soil

What colour would you call that now? That brown
which is not precisely the colour of excrement
or suede?
The depth has you hooked. Has it a scent
of its own, a peculiar adhesiveness? Is it weighed,
borne down

by its own weight? It creeps under your skin
like a landscape that's a mood, or a thought
in mid-birth,
and suddenly a dull music has begun. You're caught
by your heels in that grudging lyrical earth,
a violin

scraped and scratched, and there is nowhere to go
but home, which is nowhere to be found
and yet
is here, unlost, solid, the very ground
on which you stand but cannot visit
or know.

George Szirtes was born in Budapest in 1948, arrived in England as a refugee in 1956 and was brought up in London. He was trained as a painter in Leeds and at Goldsmiths College. He has taught art, history of art and creative writing in various schools and colleges, and currently teaches poetry and creative writing at the Norwich School of Art and Design. For some years he exhibited and ran a small etching and poetry press together with his wife, artist Clarissa Upchurch. Their children, Tom and Helen, were born and grew up in Hertfordshire.

His poems began to appear in print in the mid 70s. His first book, *The Slant Door*, was awarded the Geoffrey Faber Prize and since then he has won the Cholmondeley Award and been short-listed for the Whitbread and Forward Poetry Prizes. He was elected a Fellow of the Royal Society of Literature in 1982. Most of his books have been named as books of the year in one or other Sunday paper. He reads poems from some of these collections on *The Poetry Quartets 6* (The British Council/Bloodaxe Books, 2000), a double-cassette shared with Moniza Alvi, Michael Donaghy and Anne Stevenson.

After his first return to Hungary in 1984 he translated poetry, fiction and plays from the Hungarian and for his work in this field he has won the European Poetry Translation Prize, the Dery Prize and been shortlisted for the Weidenfeld and Aristeion Prizes as well as receiving the Golden Star medal of the Hungarian republic. His poetry is included in various contemporary anthologies and translations of his work have appeared in most European languages. He has also written for children.

His freelance work has included journalism, reviewing, radio and television. He has worked consistently for radio and much of his longer work was first broadcast on Radio Three or Four. He is very grateful for the opportunities he has been afforded to travel by the British Council. He is currently working on a novel about wrestling and co-editing the *New Writing* anthology with novelist Penelope Lively.